UGLY DUCKLING PRESSE :: DOSSIER

Sixty Morning Walks
© 2014 Andy Fitch

First Edition, First Printing
Ugly Duckling Presse
The Old American Can Factory
232 Third Street #E-303
Brooklyn, NY 11215

ISBN 978-1-937027-19-3

Distributed to the trade by
SPD / Small Press Distribution
spdbooks.org

Design by Good Utopian
Hiroshige images courtesy of the Library of Congress
Typeset in Bembo and Avenir
Printed and bound at McNaughton & Gunn
Edition of 1000

Sixty Morning Walks was fisrt published
as part of Craig Dworkin's online archive, *Eclipse*.

NATIONAL
ENDOWMENT
FOR THE ARTS

Funded in part by a grant from
the National Endowment for the Arts

uglyducklingpresse.org

Andy Fitch
SIXTY MORNING WALKS

For Kristin, from when we were young.

FOREWORD

La poésie est dans la forme des villes.
[Poetry takes the form of cities.]
—Internationale Lettriste[1]

Saunter, n. 1. Obs. rare. *? An incantation.*
—*Oxford English Dictionary*

Andy Fitch's *Sixty Morning Walks* joins a long parade of lit-
erature in a line that stretches back at least to Jean-Jacques
Rousseau's dreamy promenades and counts among its num-
ber Henry David Thoreau's plain-style walking, Charles
Baudelaire's sketchy flânneries, and Thomas de Quincey's
back-alleyway quests for a Northwest Passage. That tradi-
tion includes strolls as different as the country excursions
of the Wordsworths, Gérard de Nerval's peaceful and seri-
ous crustaceous cake-walk constitutionals, and the noctur-
nal perambulations of the Surrealists—not to mention the
fictional stalking by Edgar Allen Poe's "man of the crowd"
and the intersecting paths tracked by the wandering citi-
zens of James Joyce's Dublin.

But Fitch's text also reminds us that in addition to a lit-
erature about walking, and a literature arising from walks,
we might also identify something like a literature *of* walk-
ing—an essentially ambulant writing. Indeed, the stride
has long been a unit of literary measure (reinscribed by
the metonymy of the length of a "foot") and a model for
rhythm (with the march of metrical "feet"). At once regu-
lar and individual, walking relates the form and context of
Fitch's project. These walks cover the ground between the
narrator's impressionistic glimpses and the impersonal, uni-

form pacing of the squared numerical grid which plots the text into sixty sections of sixty sentences each.[2] In a similar way, walking functions as both the subject and structure of several scenes in Samuel Beckett's *Watt*. With his signature grammatical permutations, Beckett describes the idiosyncratic manner of Watt's "way of advancing," rigorously exhausting the possibilities for relating the members of one particular set of limbs and a rotating torso in locomotion relative to the quadrants of a compass.[3] Bruce Nauman picks up on that tension between the inherently subjective and objective measurement of the walk—its simultaneous abstractions and peculiarities—in several mid-60s works such as the descriptively titled *Walking in an Exaggerated Manner Around the Perimeter of a Square* and *Slow Angle Walk (Beckett Walk)*, in which Nauman angles the video camera 90-degrees to give the appearance that he is pacing vertically up and down the wall. This disorienting illusion underscores Nauman's precarious attempts to maintain his balance while pitching forward and backward, redistributing his center of gravity, and pivoting briskly on one foot. The risk of falling and the appearance of suspension are not coincidental to Nauman's artistic practice, and they suggest something about the genre of walking; by emphasizing the force of gravity, Nauman aligns his video performance with sculpture, which his contemporaries, at precisely that moment, were defining by its essential relation to gravity.[4] Jarrod Fowler and Shigeru Matsui have likewise both explored the generic possibilities of walking by transforming source texts into scores for perambulation and realizing pacing exercises as rhythmic, musical performances.[5]

One might, in fact, consider Fitch's work alongside any number of artistic projects from various fields in which a series of dynamic, diametric aspects intersect at the moment of ambulation: the constraint of set rules and an openness to happenstance; the individual perspective of a personal scale and the collective view of cartographic abstraction; defamiliarized surreal imagery and deadpan documentary; monotonous repetition and unpredictable adventure.[6] Those same tensions also place *Sixty Morning Walks* at the carrefour of some familiar literary trajectories, including the numerical diaristic grids of Lyn Hejinian's *My Life*, the impossible catalogue of social space surveilled by Georges Perec's *Tentative d'épuisement d'un lieu parisien,* the peripatetics of Frank O'Hara's *Lunch Poems*, and the proto-conceptual catalogue of Joe Brainard's *I Remember* series.[7] More obviously, the proximate precedents for *Sixty Morning Walks* are several of Ron Silliman's works, such as the precisely timed commuter traversal of *BART,* the sidewalk-focused catalogue of *Jones*, and the rambling narrative of *Blue*—all of which accumulate snapshot observations of public spaces and craft them into sonically torqued and radically paratactic sentences.[8] At first glance, Silliman's commonplace street-scene details appear entirely unremarkable, and like all of the works just mentioned, Fitch's text is also decidedly *pedestrian*, in both the sense of its peregrinating mode of production and its observations of everyday life. At the same time, it is *quotidian* in both senses of "routine": the workaday and the workday. As with O'Hara's lunch hour, the temporal measures of *Sixty Walks*—its careful recording of days and times in an even daily stride and a deliberate minute-by-minute step—further corresponds to an ambulatory poetics by establishing the regular rhythm of a predictable pedestrian tread within which unexpected wavers and stumbles always, wandering, occur.

If Fitch and others have undertaken a writing that approximates a kind of walking, walking in turn has itself been understood as a kind of writing. Michel de Certeau, for instance, understands "la marche [...] comme espace d'énonciation" [walking as a space of enunciation]," with its own "rhétoriques cheminatoires [footpath rhetorics]" and "énonciations piétonnières [pedestrian speech-acts]": "la marche affirme, suspecte, hasarde, transgresse, respecte, etc., les trajectoires qu'elle 'parle' [walking affirms, suspects, wagers, transgresses, respects, etc. the trajectories that it 'speaks']."[9] Moreover, walking speaks in a special way for de Certeau; it functions as a speech-act because "les traverses, dérives ou improvisations de la marche privilégient muent ou délaissent des éléments spatiaux [the oblique traversals, driftings, or improvisations of walking transform or abandon spatial elements]."[10] De Certeau's argument for the power of walking—his belief that negotiating an environment actively transforms it—echoes Henri Lefebvre's sense of space as the social production of lived experience. Space, by these definitions, is understood as something created through movement and perception among physical objects and not merely as the arrangement of monumental objects in isolation. Or, as Iain Borden, Joe Kerr, Jane Rendell and Alicia Pivar collectively put it: "architecture is not just the space-time of the permanent [....] it is also the everyday architecture of the city—that which is embedded in all the routines, activities, patterns, and emotions of quotidian life."[11]

Because space is socially produced, the particular pedestrian practices which generate that space have the potential to disrupt the monolithic urban environment conjured by the abstract ideology of "The City." The fragmented detail, in short, trumps the extensive expanse of ground that renders it legible. De Certeau, in one version of this analysis, locates such resistance at the intersection of individual subjectivity and collective community. This oppositional politics of urban walking is part of a broader discourse of post-war French theory, which privileged a specific mode of walking inextricable from a particular kind of writing: the ambient inscription of place identified as psychogeography. Guy Debord gave fair warning in the mid-50s:

> La pratique du dépaysement et le choix des rencontres, le sens de l'inachèvement et du passage, l'amour de la vitesse transposé sur le plan de l'esprit, l'invention et l'oubli sont parmi les composantes d'une *éthique de la dérive* dont nous avons déjà commencé l'expérience dans la pauvreté des villes de ce temps. / Une science des rapports et des ambiances s'élabore, que nous appelons psychogéographie

> [The practice of de-familiarization and the choice of encounters, the sense of incompleteness and transience, the love of speed transposed onto the plane of the mind, the experience of discovery and forgetting are among the elements of an *ethics of drifting* which we have already begun to test in the poverty of the cities of our time. / A science of relations and ambiences is being developed: we call it psychogeography].[12]

Relying on the idiosyncratic and irrational, the psychogeographical drift emerged from surrealist theories such as André Breton's *hasard objectif* and Salvador Dalí's *méthode paranoïaque-critique*, in which the details of the external world are seen to be unexpectedly calibrated, according to precise but unpredictable and unrecoverable formulæ, with the interior landscape of an individual psychology.[13] This legacy can be recognized in "a particular mode of constructing 'pictorial' narratives of the everyday world, rooted deeply in the insights of surrealist practices and depending on the defiant privileging of the detail over the whole, or the arbitrary juxtaposition of the mundane with the significant."[14] These pedestrian narratives evoke "not merely the urban landscape but simultaneously the existence of the narrator in that space" so that the itinerant writer "can capture just something of the subjective sensation, the sheer vividness, of urban experience and movement and perhaps hint at the 'secret history' of the city."[15]

With its tension between coherent pattern and chance, conceptual inclusiveness and individual psychology, a whiff of Situationist rhetoric lingers today in the drift of passages like the following:

> Walking is the best way to explore and exploit the city [….] Drifting is the recommended mode, trampling asphalted earth in alert reverie, allowing the fiction of an underlying pattern to assert itself. To the no-bullshit materialist this sounds suspiciously like *fin de siècle* decadence, a poetic of entropy—but the born-again flâneur is a stubborn creature, less interested in texture and fabric, eavesdropping on philosophical conversation pieces, than in noticing everything.[16]

Or, similarly:

> Walking, in particular drifting, or strolling, is already—within the speed culture of our time—a kind of resistance. Paradoxically, it's also the last private space, space from the phone or email. But it also happens to be a very immediate method or unfolding stories. [….] The walk is simultaneously the material out of which to produce art and the modus operandi of the artistic transaction. And the city always offers the perfect setting for accidents to happen.[17]

Noticing everything but retaining a trace only according to the plan of his textual map, Fitch's experiments with the relation of ambiances continue to seek the secret history of the city—with all the hallmarks of a psychogeographic science testing the ethics of the *dérive* first identified by Debord: the pedestrian traversal of an urban mise-en-scène; a narrative perspective located at the intersection of an individual's sensations and the abstraction of a collective community; surreal juxtapositions of mundane details; fragments in parataxis against the smooth rational space of gridded projections; and the subjective warp of the documentary record. Accordingly, a Situationist "rhétorique cheminatoire" echoes through the passages of *Sixty Morning Walks* like the sound of footsteps circumambulating the arcades of a city on the verge of disappearing in the twilight of a culture that has almost forgotten, in its haste to traipse, to venture itself with a saunter.

—Craig Dworkin

NOTES

1 "Réponse à une enquête du groupe surréaliste belge," *Potlatch* 5 (20 juillet, 1954).

2 And further: into a projected sixty-part series spanning sixty-years, including the cracked transcriptions of *Sixty Morning Wlaks* [sic] and the interviews of *Sixty Morning Talks*, which are being issued concurrently with the present volume.

3 Samuel Beckett: *Watt* (New York: Grove, 1953): 30.

4 See, for instance, Robert Morris: "Notes on Sculpture: Part I," *Artforum* 4: 6 (February, 1966): 43, as well as the praxis of Carl Andre's "carpet" pieces.

5 Consider, for example, Jarrod Fowler's 2008 performance *Drumming, Beating, Striking (Transportation as Rhythm)*, (Non-Event, Axiom Gallery, Boston), and Shigeru Matsui's 2003 performance *Pure Poem Walking* (Toyota Municipal Museum of Art).

6 Some of the most salient examples include: Richard Long's 1967 *A Line Made by Walking*; Hamish Fulton's description of himself as "a walking artist"; Francis Alÿs's documented *paseos* of the 1990s, including *The Paradox of Practice 1 (Sometimes Making Something Leads to Nothing)* (1997); Janet Cardiff's *Forest Walk* (Banff, 1991) and subsequent audio tours; Stanley Brouwn's *This Way Brouwn* (1960-1964) and *A Distance of 336 Steps* (Amsterdam: Netherlands Foundation for Visual Arts, Design and Architecture, 2000); Sandra Rechico's *Whereabouts* (Toronto: Parasitic Ventures Press, 2007); Sophie Calle's *Suite vénitienne* (Seattle: Bay Press, 1988); Vito Acconci's *Following Piece* (1969); *et cetera*. For a wider spectrum of related projects see Karen O'Rourke: *Walking and Mapping: Artists as Cartographers* (Cambridge: MIT, 2013).

7 Lyn Hejinian: *My Life* (Providence: Burning Deck, 1980; expanded edition Los Angeles: Sun & Moon, 1987; expanded edition as *My Life and My Life in the Nineties*, Middletown: Wesleyan University Press, 2013); Georges Perec: *Tentative d'épuisement d'un lieu parisien* (Paris: Union générale d'éditions, 1975); Frank O'Hara: *Lunch Poems*, Pocket Poets Series 19 (San Francisco: City Lights, 1964); Joe Brainard: *I Remember* (New York: Angel Hair, 1970; expanded collection New York: Granary, 2001).

8 Ron Silliman: *BART* (Hartford: Potes & Poets, 1982); "Blue," in *Paris Review* 86 (Winter 1982): 84-88, and as part of *ABC* (Berkeley: Tuumba, 1983); *Jones* (Mentor: Generator, 1993).

9 Michel de Certeau: *L'invention du quotidien 1. Arts de faire* (Paris, Gallimard, 1990): 148; 151; 150.

10 *Ibidem*, 154.

11 Iain Borden, Joe Kerr, Jane Rendell and Alicia Pivar (Editors): *The Unknown City: Contesting Architecture and Social Space* (Cambridge: MIT, 2000): 10.

12 Guy Debord pour L'Internationale Lettriste: "Réponse à la question: 'La pensée nous éclaire-t-elle, et nos actes, avec la même indifférence que le soleil, ou quel est notre espoir et quelle est sa valeur?,' *La Carte d'après nature* (juin, 1954), in Debord, *Œuvres* (Paris: Gallimard, 2006): 120.

13 André Breton: *L'Amour fou* (Paris: Gallimard, 1937); note the pathway [*chemin*] in Breton's most explicit definition of the concept, which links his understanding of chance back to the novel's narrative of urban wanderlust: "Le hasard serait la forme de manifestation de la nécessité extérieure qui se fraie un chemin dans l'inconscient humain [Chance takes the form of the manifestation of the external necessity that traces a path for itself in the human unconscious]"; Salvador Dalí: "Aspects phénoménologiques de la methode paranoiaque-critique," *Oui* (Paris: Gonthier, 1971):'39-52.

14 Borden et *alii, Unknown City*, 19.

15 *Ibidem*. The fragments of juxtaposed detail underwriting the secret history of the city recalls the "secret" actualization of fragments in Roland Barthes' description of the walker as a kind of reader in a passage quoted by de Certeau (who is quoting Claude Soucy quoting Barthes): "L'usager de la ville prélève des fragments de l'énoncé pour les actualiser en secret [the user of a city selects certain fragments of the statement in order to actualize them in secret]." See Roland Barthes: "Sémiologie et urbanisme," *L'Architecture d'aujourd'hui* 153 (December 1970 - January 1971): 11-13.

16 Iain Sinclair: *Lights Out for the Territory* (London: Penguin, 2003): 4.

17 Francis Alÿs, "Interview" (with Russell Ferguson), *Francis Alÿs*, ed. Cuauhtémoc Medina (London: Phaidon, 2007): 31.

SIXTY MORNING WALKS

It must all be considered as if spoken by a character in a novel

—Roland Barthes

I watched the wind billow, fabric unfurl.

TUESDAY 2.15

Before I pulled back the curtain I knew it was raining but then a sparrow called and I knew I'd been wrong. Bright clouds blew across the courtyard shaft. My New Balance had to stay stuffed with paper. My jeans had dried hung in the shower and didn't even itch.

Two women opened Dana Discovery Center. The one driving a golf cart in circles stopped. Silent attraction flowed between us. The other smoked and rinsed rubber floormats. Wind made it cold for khaki ecologist suits.

A cross-eyed girl shouted Morning! I couldn't tell if there was someone behind me. On the way past I said Hello, twice, but she stared off gulping air. The pond at 110th (The Harlem Meer) gets so reflective sometimes. Christo's Gates had been up since Saturday. Last night I'd finally got to see them (in dismal circumstances: heavy bag, broken umbrella, damp socks and gloves).

In all the Conservatory Gardens only one cluster of snowdrops had bloomed. Slender green shoots looked strong. Patchy light came through the trellis.

As a jogger emitting techno beats curved beyond the baseball fields I thought about vicarious emotional momentum. She had glossy dark hair. So many people use expensive hair products now.

Somebody with leashes wrapped around one wrist sat with his face in a Daily News. People must always bug him about what it's like to be a dog walker. No squirrels in sight, I noted, because of storms. I was forgetting my initial discomfort with Christo's drapes (of course they have to be durable). I watched the wind billow, fabric unfurl. It felt like standing under women's thighs.

Three poodles passed while I stood thinking. The drabbest of them looked up. It drew in breath but just shivered. Sirens helped maintain a muffled morning feeling. I pictured a neighbor hearing it all from his room—under blankets with the window open. I waited for a brownish jay to pivot. I guess I really wanted a blue jay. A heart-shaped balloon staggered between currents, sailed across East Meadow airspace.

A tattered ice sheet seemed about to split from The Pool's shore. (In the Conservatory Gardens bulletin bin I'd found a complimentary Central Park Anniversary Map & Guide subtitled *150 Years Of Strolling: Priceless*. That's where I'm getting all these proper names.) Always at least one mallard paused, staring out where water began. Inevitably the bird would plop except that word's not right; this was all very quiet.

A setter winked while carrying a crooked stick. I wanted to say It looks like he's smoking a pipe but didn't know if the dog was a he or she. This occurred as I wound up Great Hill (West 104th). By then the park had filled with compact invigorated people. Frizzy high-school girls sped south. The blonde's make-up resembled a charcoal sketch. For the second time this morning I wondered why I can't hold my gaze on unattractive strangers (just to be polite).

Most moms wore jackets not a raincoat like me. (When I'd first crossed 110th, at 8:06, cars' tires kicked up iridescent dew so that they looked stationary for a second, like fountains.) The muddiest stretches weren't soggy anymore. In the North Woods large white men leaned against a golf cart dozing. Both flinched when I appeared. I willed myself to make eye contact, just to will something, but my stare never left the trail.

Skirting Lenox I almost collided with a woman when boys refused to step beyond crosswalk paint. I felt jammed, and, amid the confusion, saw the sign for Second Canaan Baptist Church. I'd voted for president at Second Canaan, had never looked in that direction since.

Back inside (9:12) it sounded like an aviary. Now (10:10) there's only one periodic caw. Our showerhead's leaking. Lamps hang tilted in the window reflection.

WEDNESDAY

Kristin says my metabolism will slow if I don't eat until after walking and writing about it: so first a quick bowl of yogurt, granola, almonds.

Kristin woke us around 8:15. Both eyes looked puffy when I put in contacts. Dahlias spread before me as the elevator opened. I held the door for neighbors and an Eskimo dog. We said Hi but never looked at each other— my vision just blurred to the left. It was unseasonably hot (like every winter now) on Greenwich. One coffee-carrying woman wore a creamy bell-shaped dress and housefly sunglasses. Her heels tied at the ankles.

All down Murray cabs kept slamming shut; I only noticed because there weren't any sirens. I appreciated that standpipes look so brassy and antique. In a warehouse someone slid cases of Coke and Sprite off a handcart. Somebody with a hard hat tucked a blueprint in his pocket. Delivery guys on West St. relaxed in the front of a warm bright van. The driver laid his boots along the dashboard. A Post sprawled in his lap. 12 year-olds pranced by in boutique denim.

Powerball tickets clotted a puddle. Sprayed orange arrows pointed across the river. The Hudson rocked a bit—wrinkled, calm. Saws buzzed all around me. To the right stood a raw uneven stump with someone straddling its limbs. Along the Irish Hunger Memorial arcs of aspens lay toppled. A tree had been boxed by a wooden scaffold. I turned to the water and tried to speak spontaneously and this is basically what came: New Jersey you can be so hard to see, though your air caresses my face, reminding me I have one, but why must it feel like a leather mask?

A Starbucks cup would have blown in the harbor if it hadn't been left almost full. Commuters disembarked from a Hoboken Ferry. The men looked symmetrical (how they dressed). The women's clicking heels made it hard to glance at them and concentrate. Pylons leaned against each other resembling nymphs or redwoods.

I slowed passing fir trees. The Holocaust Memorial site sat quiet. Geese picked through its fenced-off yard.

Right where the Battery curves, right where you can see storms coming or the edge of night, someone with a big skull stood wanting to say hello. I said Good morning (first, so it wouldn't seem reciprocal). Sun spread across his face. No words came from him. A man reading the Wall Street Journal also reminded me of sun. A lot of benches looked freshly painted, wet even, wind-streaked. Branches had budded way too early.

Bronze hands reached out from the river. Somebody thrust above her bangs a plastic replica of the Liberty torch. Someone spray-painted copper green straddled her. Souris! the girl's mother cried. But she just stared, austere and proud, posing less for her parents than her own children. Arabic men arranged pretzel carts. Particular shelves produced steamy puffs, like warm patches you come across swimming. Silhouettes crossed Staten Island Ferry windows.

On the way back someone bowed and chanted amid circles of D-sized batteries. A tidy Native American slept. He sat almost straight, wore woolen gloves. Garbage bags rested along his thighs.

Closer to Murray somebody olive-skinned had huge white blotches between his nose and mouth. I only stared on my second chance (right when we passed). I thought I heard frogs. It was the warning sound as garage gates shut. A chauffeur rushed from the Resident Suites apologizing. A porter yelled Remove your vehicle. I stepped too deeply off the curb. A bubble in my back got twisted.

THURSDAY

After bhindi masala I awoke with shaky bowels. Bring two dollars I thought, while rinsing a contact, in case there's a bathroom for customers only. But at the corner I realized I'd forgotten the money.

I'd never gone east from our apartment and so at 8:06 I turned that way. Cops tilted chins to check me out through facemasks. I tried to imprint on my memory people's posture at the bus stop, the way Degas would. I crossed beneath an LIRR—right where a boy once shocked my ex-roommate with a sticky, pushy slap that strained his neck. During one crazy gust a garbage bag and I bound towards each other like long lost friends. There were few broken bottles, more milk-top rings. There were waves of children's laughter but no visible kids.

:rmarket discount pages lay frozen. In a puddle
ıst headline: The Lyin' King. A Caribbean woman
 v it was her 9-year-old goddaughter could explain
sex. Parents walked as far as a school gate. Beyond the fence
mini basketballs flew almost always without the necessary
arc. Sparrows zigzagged around stiff adults. Four girls and
one boy squatted tearing paper, discussing life.

From a dusty park of mismatch chairs poked a Puerto
Rican flag (which I always confuse with Texas). Locked
to tall crates sat a fifteen-foot tricycle painted like a grass-
hopper. Its plastic cover ripped where wind pressed against
peddles.

Fringe flapped outside a deli as a woman stepped
down, slow but intrepid on her three-pronged cane. A
tossed mattress depicted fauna where it wasn't torn by coil.
All around stone crumbled. White people smirked. None
seemed attractive.

110th ended on Thomas Jefferson Park: just baseball
diamonds and a corridor. A squirrel stared then panicked.
With traffic purring and the sky absent of color winter in the
city felt calm and private. Across a footbridge the East River
stirred, glimmering and consistent, thick but not unclean.
Across water I saw more fences—Riker's Island maybe.
Below, a man with an afro chased his german shepherd. It
felt like a seagull's point of view (there weren't any).

I couldn't understand Ward's Island Bridge unless
there was a hidden elevator or stairs. Something told me
That bridge is useless; enjoy this humble pier. Yet I con-
tinued south, neglecting the pier. Only when a cormorant
popped up did I realize nothing had been happening for a
while, and even then the syllables for cormorant wouldn't
cohere in my head. Another bird, some type of Japanese

duck, stark white with jagged orange and gray, slipped off
the embankment. It shook strands of fuzz from its beak to
better peck at the river surface. You are beautiful I cried.
The closest pigeons spread dramatically striped tail-feath-
ers. What is all this? I asked one. A pair of Indian men
stopped to retie shoes. I disliked overtaking them that way.

A project's yard stood filled with plastic animals: holy
deer kneeling, elephants and owls. When I slowed to look
a live great dane bore down on me like a stallion. Several
blocks later I read an unofficial plaque mounted to one
handball court. The boy in the photo appeared gaunt and
pony-tailed. There was a poem or something lineated in
Spanish. Without fully pausing I resumed my vigorous
pace, felt guilty for grinning as I'd approached this shrine.

A lot of balconies had hanging bikes. Others were
stuffed with washed-out boxes. On my walk back to
Central Park I trailed an old akita and a woman crying.
Christo's Gates split it all into a thousand fresh particles. I
joined the informal press tour.

In the Conservatory Gardens two tree trunks got
sawed. I wondered if we'll face an arboreal blight so far only
discussed in the Metro Section. For some reason I wouldn't
ask the groundskeeper. I inspected logs in her pick-up. Many
felt hollow. On the way through trellises, down toward the
lawn, I saw a blue jay then a sultry female cardinal.

FRIDAY

From the gloom I couldn't find my phone (my "watch").
At 8:32 for the first time ever I turned up Lenox (Malcolm
X). Solids became outlines blasted with sun. My eyes

wouldn't grasp anything specific. Soon children streamed by in well-organized columns bearing bright, well-sculpted faces. A cat arched its spine in a laundromat window. A green Lincoln with hazards flashing roared then swerved around me. A maroon Cadillac's taillight blinked as if the alarm was about to sound. Pigeon flocks swirled overhead and I felt curved and scattered. One stray feather straggled behind.

Letters in the sign for Lloyd Toppin Funeral Home hung tilted crooked like funny teeth. As I approached 125th the way one bus driver filled her pants seemed hypnotizing (but not sexual). Lampposts looked huge against blank sky. Barehanded Latino boys passed each other sinks. Somebody peeked from a window with tubes up his nostrils. Sparrows could be heard everywhere.

I'd started to feel menaced by looming projects. A mom looked both admiring and afraid of the pit bull she pushed her daughter past. This close-cropped dog somehow turned me on. Kids wore bandannas beside a Checks Cashed place. But in the next band of so-called intimidating kids the fiercest bragged about acing biology. Crowds flowed off the subway steps. The "menacing projects" were a Columbia hospital. The city had grown faceless.

To the west lay several wiry parks (Morningside, St. Nicholas). I was moving slowly: 25 blocks in 20 minutes. It wasn't even that slow a pace but I told myself it was. I told a pigeon You are imperturbable.

When my eyes began tearing I said Hello to one family. An elderly woman stepped down her stoop. I paused so she could continue without fear of a crash. She stopped, smiled, waved me on.

Dead firs stood embayed in black iron plots but how beautiful, always, near St. Nick's. I passed a Make My Cake bakery and realized it's a chain. A plaque celebrated benevolent doctors. Another recalled the story of Striver's Row. I wondered if I'd made a spectacle of myself, standing around reading while the block gentrified. City College now looked Teutonic. Too bad there was no brook to cross.

Puffy boys peered out from trails' ends. I couldn't see their faces. Police tape whipped around in benches. A light toe-press burst air pockets lacing one puddle, so that after these exquisite cracks ice remained and my shoes weren't wet.

A retired Filipino kicked his floppy dogs forward as they lay bewildered on the frozen lawn. Something about how this man's clothes fit suggested satisfaction with life. The park seemed to have been designed so you wouldn't notice leaving. I stepped on nail clippers. Flurries picked up.

On the way home I went berserk—letting traffic dictate what streets I took. I've needed new shoes since December but only today did my foot soles start ripping. Men refurbished a townhouse without any facade. The clouds were just more brownstones. I wanted to scream Soon we will be moving into such clouds! but by then sidewalks felt packed. The first of many sirens rang. The only yard I saw would have been big enough to lie in if not for a sewer.

Back on Lenox African names brought pleasure but commercial signs quickly corroded my sense of self. Back on my own block somebody asked the muttering white person ahead to purchase a Final Call. No one asked me. Workers dragged pipes to the building next door. So this spring also there will be intense construction.

The snowballs I dropped floated instead of melting.

MONDAY

As I spun out Kristin's door my cheeks dampened. At 8:20
sidewalks looked like crisco. Someone dragged three big
boxes of salt behind him, enough for decades of storms.
A driver honked accidentally then stared to her left. A
bus for the elderly got packed in by plows. Gulls dropped
from gray sky like flurries, sounding human, dangling feet.
Others kept their feet tucked (which I've always found so
elegant).

Jigs blasted from the Hunger Memorial's camou-
flaged speakers. Songs gave way to shrill oration. A jogger
strained to shout Morning through frosted monument posts.
Following his slippery progress I ended up surrounded by
waist-high concrete. Tire tracks coiled like spiral vertebrae.
I studied my own tracks then, turning forwards, sensed I
might collide with somebody and flinched.

The Hudson coursed—high and busy. The snow-
balls I dropped floated instead of melting. Lapping sounds
bubbled up the embankment. Purple feathers swept by as if
two pigeons were being plucked. New Jersey's skyline stood
charcoal, truncated. Halfway out a cormorant gleamed.

Crossing North Cove Cherry Orchard boots I'd
found in the recycling bin grew saturated and heavy. Some
branches hung crowned with tiny pinhead buds. Some of
these buds lay beaded and glistening. Exposed birds' nests
entwined paper-products wound with withered stems. I
paused to watch opaque sky through branches. A ruddy
person veered off to the right. I said At least these fresh
brown ovals punctuate the scene. But I didn't say it loud
enough to make the man or muzzled husky stop.

Pine boughs sagged along the Esplanade. Only piers
looked geometric. Through mist a bright orange ferry

scuttled toward Staten Island. Garbage swirled, never leaving South Cove. A ladybug-patterned kickball rocked against the mossy river line. Nearby stirred foamy bubbles, jagged wood, bags.

An exquisite box lay slightly off center in the frost-rimmed Wagner Fountain basin. A boy assumed his mother just pretended to spot the Statue of Liberty.

Follow my finger.

I told you I *see* it!

After half a regular walk I'd already turned around. My mind felt glazed. I was thinking of how I no longer like the broad lapels on my one suit.

Later I plunged down unplowed steps, tried to feel my way back into morning. I toured the embankment that lines North Cove. Police had forbidden this in the past but seemed bound to be more lenient today. Water spread in three directions. Seagulls stood poised atop each post that demarcates the harbor. The closest bird cocked its head at me. I asked How can you stand on such brittle legs? Why are your eyes so red?

Amid repressed father/son snowball fights finally appeared one Mexican family shrieking. When the dad pointed his camera toward the river two children slid and made slushy angels. The mom bopped her husband on the forehead, demanded he take a photo of the kids. Much of this was comically enacted for my benefit. Facemasked police weighed the scene down at its corners. As always their machine guns looked more like silhouettes.

On the return up Murray I watched a Diamond Meats truck sink back into a hotel garage. A tall blonde talking on her phone crossed the intersection oblivious of traffic. My voice wouldn't come—as it often won't in dreams. Cabs honked and skidded. The woman passed speaking some Scandinavian language. This blended with my mental picture of fjords.

TUESDAY

As we descended at 8:06 Kristin said my most annoying trait is shoes coming untied. Ahead in the lobby a woman walked on crutches. Emilia from the drycleaner's smiled through glass. Stacked Wall Street Journals leaned against the store devoted to mailing things. My friend Jon's mountain boots felt like tourniquets around my ankles.

Kristin kissed me in front of Ceci Cela. I strode through tabloids pressed semi-transparent. A phone booth stood dripping. So did awnings and scaffolds. Birdcalls sounded unusually like drips. Where whiteness fluttered to my left a Popeye's Chicken employee washed windows. He flinched at our nearness. He had cornrows. Across Broadway a tan woman turned so the fruit guy could stuff her backpack. There was nowhere else to look: all lunch-hour discount boards, bus stop Perry Ellis advertisements and hip-hop posters stapled to construction. An unused courthouse's carved figures suggested wind and spring.

I've never understood if Chambers ends on City Hall, or at least the new City Hall, or if official City Hall remains the Federalist compound with a park in back. Beneath stone towers I came upon a roadblock/police hut. A woman swept through screened by bushes. I followed into a relaxing plaza. Police cadets picked at bakery, circled each other like sparrows.

A second gate appeared with winding stalls (reminiscent of public pools). I'd made it through when someone yelled:

Hey! photo I.D.

Half-spinning around I said I just want to get back to Broadway.

You *can't* two guards said simultaneously.

What am I supposed to do then stand here all morning?

Sir step to the entrance and wait for me there.

A guard emerged from the hut, told me I'd need to be escorted out. She changed her mind and pointed down a stairwell. That way and left, on the *far* side she said. You're not al*lowed* in here.

I don't want to *be* in here I said, then worried she'd radio for backup, then I'd hit Madison heading east. Crossing St. James I wanted to check out a van where I heard somebody rip his chewy bagel apart. I lost myself amid mint-green characters on the back of Asian seafood trucks. I wondered which garden-level salons ever open.

Across Canal stood the chrome-plated cube that used to be a good dance club. I realized I'd just passed an ex-girlfriend's block. When I swerved back towards Market one woman assumed I was stalking her. We strode ahead unable to separate. Finally I stopped and tried to determine if the bird above me was a grackle. My vision grew weak, especially on details, but I loved looking through webs of branches at sky.

Passing Abby's I pictured a chaotic bedroom with amiable sighing Manhattan Bridge traffic. Mysterious podiums still fronted her hallway. As I looped back taking an alley a random parked Saab seemed sinister. Rutgers, LaGuardia and Viadeck homes seemed solid, even with spilled plastic bags outside them: purple-brown sportcoats fluttered on ice.

Between signals pigeons pecked at crosswalk. Plaques commemorated a mission run off Henry. I immediately forgot the founders' names—it's so hard to remember that New York. Hasid boys framed by iron grids stopped skipping when they felt me pause. A middle-aged Chinese guy strolled down Division in sweatpants and flip-flops, not at all cold. An old man pushed a delivery door. It budged. Surprised, he called for two women at street-level to follow him down. They glanced at me, embarrassed. People boarded an idling bus to Boston. The next minute consisted of slowly passing an enormous crowded fruit stand.

I followed someone limping (crossed more police checkpoints). A sign in front of the New Amsterdam Public Library said Sorry We Do Not Accept Donations At This Time, so I sifted through books left along the lobby, selected a Rand McNally publication entitled *Around the World: a view from space:* Authentic Gemini Photographs. It showed pictures taken from an altitude of 400 miles, captions describing "the drama of Fukien Province (Mainland China) at left, and southwestern Taiwan (Formosa)." The book still smells of pepper/cologne. I'm hoping pages won't stick when it dries.

WEDNESDAY

After lying in bed sad starting at 4:58 I stepped out at 8:29. Beyond the courtyard big clouds streamed west. The wind resembled what I hear when I yawn. The one tree on our block stood hunched under scaffolds. Batteries and a blue lighter nestled in its plot. Two boys turned where Lenox was extra bright. Coherently dressed people looked calm without gloves so I tried taking mine off.

Small brown tassels dangled from sycamores. The Siberian elm just had two limbs cut. I wished more trees carried identification cards. A redhead back pedaling on a fold-up bike created a pleasant gear-grinding sound. A gas station (Frederick Douglass) dispersed my morning focus. It was filled with taxis. Concrete tubes lay stacked in pyramids. Steam swelled curbside recycling bags.

Papery leaves along the Morningside Park fence confirmed a strong, consistent wind. Sparrows sped through fence gaps until one perched there. Both seemed better for it. I skated across snow crust. Ice covered the park's official wildlife pond, cordoned off with Caution tape. Stray yellow ribbons rocked underwater. Fallen branches tore the stair rail. Footprints melted.

Atop 112th a woman smiled. She shivered beside a locked academic building. I didn't slow down. I didn't have keys. Her face slackened. Women clipped by in brittle-sounding heels. One must have assumed I was looking at her sexually. She seemed to half-torque to give me a full frontal view unconsciously.

At two consecutive coffee/bagel stands relaxed customers joked with cashiers. These were established morning rituals. There was a garden-level bakery I'll sometime try. Croissant trays cooled by the propped back door.

Part of St. John's steps stood roped. More snow bunched here than the rest of the city. On the way in I tensed preparing for a bag search. Dim lamps dangled from construction scaffolds. The nave smelled like sun and dust.

The stained glass didn't seem so garish. A thick boy with a buzz cut sobbed. A woman listened with her hand on his arm. Kids on fieldtrips crossed paths but didn't intermingle or really notice each other. They must have been in different grades.

Crossing Amsterdam I felt calm, uncertain I'd make it to the other side. I followed several pigeons until the Hudson lay below—impossible to reach. A staircase led one tier closer to the river. I started towards a craggy overhang. I and a pair of joggers kept hesitating to avoid a collision until we all stopped pretty frustrated with each other. Afterwards I spun around. Tipped trash bins stayed padlocked. Bikes locked along a dumplings restaurant held multiple plastic bags tied to seats.

Climbing West End I studied a sycamore tassel. I found a better one and dropped the first. It took time sliding down: much farther than expected.

On the shortcut path through Central Park a young couple kissed in Christo vests. I felt in a pocket to confirm I had keys, pricked my finger on sycamore pods. For most of this walk I'd been thinking about the future (completely unobservant).

THURSDAY

At 9:27 sky was white. A street-sweeping vehicle brushed near me. Letters in my gloved hand were all I could think about—or else I'd forget to mail them.

Beige grass stood where snow had melted. Ice shards clung to bent-over reeds. Christo's assistants gathered beyond The Meer's edge. They'd unknowingly formed a perfect crescent. Park benches looked long and left me tired, like train tracks.

A mom slowed to let me pass in case I was a creep. A lhasa apso sniffing The Meer got dragged back towards cement. A woman pumped expensive cross-country ski poles. For four consecutive blocks I only saw females. Wavy tiles along Fifth Ave. hurt my shins. I was disappointed with myself for not visiting a Joseph Albers retrospective at the Museum of Design. I forgot to look when passing the Jewish Museum (I'd been reading about the Primary Structures show). At just the right moment I turned to catch Ward's Island Bridge stretch away from Spanish Harlem.

Stylish blonds near the Guggenheim got hydraulically lifted to the back of a truck. Across Fifth a security guard gathered herself. She lined her dashboard with stuffed animals.

Two businesswomen cruised down 86th hoping to catch a bus dropping people at the curb. I cheered for them until one sidestepped the most innocuous puddle. Briefly we became synchronized, with the bus pulling forwards and her headed to the back. Students on a fieldtrip marched between us. A girl was able to run, smile and hold hands with friends walking at a normal pace. Her purple hat said CATHERINE.

A big family declined to cross 85th because of flashing signals. I could only wedge around them by flattening a pizza box. Climbing towards The Met my vision never adjusted to a second tier of stone steps perpendicular to the first. Old couples argued if they should enter. The clerk craned her neck and held a palm out for my nickel: I watched her pupils expand.

I quickly crossed the Byzantine rooms, barely lingering on icons. Turning left amid terracotta sculptures I skirted the giant Choir Screen. In a thick Argentine accent an elevator operator announced Exit at rear. Exit at rear! he told a Korean woman, who saw no reason to turn while we were rising. When we all stepped out she was the only one to thank him.

From the roof garden Christo's Gates still didn't overwhelm me. Park lay obscured by additions to the architecture. Barren branches all seemed the same height. This was a view for evening, with people chatting as you gaze outwards.

Back on the ground I couldn't help pausing beside a lacquered-oak cabinet overlaid with ebony. A humid smell amid Arts of Africa and Oceania seemed somehow familiar. As I left I got to pass my favorite guard (she looks just like Sugar Ray Leonard), but otherwise this hadn't been the morning I'd intended; I meant to see the Rubens drawings.

Back along Fifth one Mayan nanny could barely reach high enough to steer her stroller. A woman waiting to have a wheelchair hoisted called friends from the bus stop. There was some awkward delay. There were stuffed tigers strung to the back of the wheelchair. Shaggy Japanese girls kept exiting a cab until a male slid out and shut the door.

The rich lady with ski poles cut me off again, behind an entrance to the jogging track. She bounced waiting for a walk sign—carried on funny conversations with somebody's schnauzer. In a car around 100th St. a couple twisted and faced an old woman. All three wore thick wool coats and looked spent. A girl's sweatpants read CALIFORNIA across the butt. Someone collecting recyclables nodded my way. I wondered if I had stared too long. Only as I left the park did I remember bags of bottles lining our curb.

From the farthest courtyard I cut back to clarify what today had been about. Women waiting for a bus resented my reappearance. Sparrows scrubbed themselves in a dry dirt plot. It was sort of raining.

FRIDAY

From the furthest lobby door in our building hangs a red Locknetics button you have to press. I paused there to collect myself. I wanted morning to crash against me like a wave (Marcus Aurelius). The door popped open at 8:06. The sky got bluer higher up. Puffy snow ringed garbage bins. Luis and Frankie (the superintendent and the assistant super) shoveled crooked paths. Frankie still wore his tiny leather jacket.

Every stoop had someone outside it shoveling. Extra salt kept getting tossed. I'd never noticed that Pentecostal churches have such gigantic crosses. A few churches cut trails from the street to their steps. Along others men chopped at ice with spade-like things.

An M-4 skidded beyond Duke Ellington Circle. I yelled as if yelling through the driver's window but already the bus had passed me by. Somebody selling wet Posts from the sidewalk winked. I wasn't at all kind to this man.

The abandoned boots I'd worn weren't working out. Still I dropped down Madison curious where the Upper East Side starts. A teenage girl looked calm without winter gear. A housing complex reeked of garlic. A pizza place sold garlic knots three for a buck. When I slowed to see what a garlic knot was it felt like pedestrians might smother me (the heavy security guard made some catty comment).

In the low 100's a woman slouched, annoyed, waiting for her sister to catch up on a cane. I've got a lot of shit on my mind the younger sibling told pedestrians. I crossed an intersection unconsciously and happened to be lucky the light was green.

Just as I thought, Spanish Harlem or the ghetto, or whatever my neighborhood is ends with a hospital—Mt. Sinai at 99th. Equally predictable: architecture changes immediately but you wait 2 blocks before white folks start. At first it became blinding like a ski slope. A parking-lot attendant wore earmuffs in his shed. Tabloids said the pope would soon die. The Times focused on our fraught relations with Russia.

Arrows pointed down a plywood corridor. Dark bricks dropped into a shuddering vat. Soon there were bakeries. I wanted an almond tart. As I glanced in a diner someone studied its enormous menu through bifocals. A twelve-year-old with cream-colored tastes hailed a cab. His curly hair glistened. He was tan.

My toes chafed against the boots' suede tongues. A chauffeur led a handsome couple to the curb. All expressed relief turning up Park Ave. Bright trees stood budding and there weren't many stores. I halted to let an au pair hoist Chinese kids whenever they reached a puddle. I fixated on stenciled reminders to curb your dog. A vista was coming around 96th. A doorman swept at slush with his broom. Another talked to himself but it wasn't anti-social. A cleaning woman stopped to ask about his children.

I descended without anything to see (with even housing projects turned away). Two Long Island trains crossed paths shaving snow from the rails like bobsleds. I squatted 12 blocks from home with throbbing ankles. I cut west early looking for distraction. Shovelers leaned on handles now, talking.

Christo's Gates looked lonely and pure. A flier announced a mid-March rally to end the war. The song "Whenever you call me, I'll be there" was in my head and then I heard it on the lobby radio. Our lobby—I'd never noticed—has really nice tiles.

Maybe I'd sensed them coming.

MONDAY

Kristin and I exited at 8:18. It was balmy while the door revolved, cold outside. We split apart at Warren under a grating sparrow. There'd been a fire at Baluchi's—all the trash looked charred. All down Murray only electric things were bright. Then a businessman turned a corner with his pug in a pink shawl.

I squeezed myself against big gusts, often on the verge of giggling. Kristin's neighbor Carol crossed not dressed right for the cold. When she waved, my arm wouldn't rise past the shoulder. Photographs hovered facedown on Church. Salt deposits left the sidewalk patchy. At the intersection's midpoint a woman and her son paused. There, he said, can you smell it? The Empire State Building peeked out as I sniffed.

I felt tall and stunned crossing through the glare. I wanted to take off gloves and reach for pigeons. Chris (the doorman) appeared ahead discussing Japanese cutlery. A cop stood beside every subway station, a chorus of walkie-talkie chatter. Sirens and light converged several blocks south down Broadway. City Hall Park's masonite slabs stayed slippery even in new sneakers. The public-art project continued to expand: from people to cows to taxis. An Arabic boy threw snaps at my shins and his parents didn't care. Scarf pressed against my Adam's apple.

Stalled opposite the Brooklyn Bridge I wondered which crossing guards do any good. Commuters dropping down the pedestrian-ramp seemed emotionally someplace else. One read a slender New York Times. A sign warned No Salt Past This Point but it wasn't true; there were streams of salt. I climbed past the Murry Bergtraum High School for Business Careers and boring residential towers. I crossed above where the F.D.R. drips freeway grime on people's faces. As glowing women passed one stared intently, the way I stare.

One yellow pedestrian icon disintegrated into blah pavement flakes. A woman stepped back to photograph this. I weaved but my shoe still scattered her shot. The East River glistened through planks underfoot. A Staten Island Ferry cut across the bay. I slowed before an engineering diagram and read it all without absorbing. A string of Valentine balloons had gotten entangled in bridge cables. A silent D-train descended toward Chinatown. So much else sat stationary. Like always Brooklyn Heights looked flush. I was happy not to live in some endless field.

Turning back, Manhattan stood monumental but I didn't feel pressure to acknowledge this (dulled by traffic rush on either side). Lyric poems had been chalked into benches. Nobody strained to read the tiny letters. One couple ahead wore dark-hued jeans. I began to swerve around them. A biker rang his bell.

From Park Row I got caught in commuter streams off the 4-5-6. The pace grew brisk but mournful. The man in front kept glancing behind his shoulder. On my way past City Hall Park fountain I realized all its plants are potted—how discouraging. Somebody awoke along a nondescript Irish tavern. He glared at the menus in his hand.

Portabello's Sicilian Kitchen smelled fresh today. They must have had the ovens cleaned. The plaster chef advertising pizza/soda combos pointed stubbed fingers like an ancient statue. His butt made me picture George Grosz paintings. The Vietnamese mother bent to shine black boys' shoes. Her shop is part of Kristin's building. Why do I think of them as separate?

TUESDAY

Temper tantrum around 8:15—couldn't find a hat. Then slid plastic bags between my shoes and socks. Only thin trails had been shoveled. Cutting into Central Park I grabbed a handful of snow off somebody's fender, sprinkled this like a chef. A goose spun in circles, floating, asleep. Christo's Gates were gone.

Across The Meer two silhouettes looked small tossing snow on water. Behind them used to stand Fort Clinton: strategic site held by the British during the Revolutionary War, the U.S. in 1812 (I read signs about it 20 minutes later). I climbed the North Woods crunching snow, following dogprints. Today it felt like there were extra trees. Snow only covered trunks' northwest quadrants. I pictured Jean Dubuffet, Japanese paper houses and a lampshade of my grandma's. At the bluff's top someone had left bicycle treads.

From Rustic Bridge No. 31 the pine-bough reflection looked lithographed. Occasionally a snowflake spread rings across it. This was exquisite beauty and thinking that thought didn't get in the way. Just when I decided to move, a woman and a corgie appeared. Maybe I'd sensed them coming.

I followed The Loch worried I'd get spit out at an ugly intersection. For a while waterfalls crashed ahead. Twigs turned into cold brown mulch. People carried disposable cameras—mostly men looking awkward in jeans and sneakers. Joggers had claimed a plowed road. Pores on my face felt wide apart.

The approaching dogs sounded familiar. So did their owners' voices. One woman narrated the scene: He's good at breaking loose; oh, now he's cornered. I envisioned these words drifting across outer space. I checked maps and discerned where The Reservoir was. Apparently the American Gum's the other tree (besides sycamores) with tassels. As I traversed a slushy ditch a cross-country skier called Another winter wonderland! The phrase left me blank.

I'd twisted my ankle early on and was starting to become aware of this. I leaned against the Reservoir gate imagining conversations about snow with somebody French. Beyond the water's silky crust a pair of what I'm calling Asian cormorants dove one after the other. I felt a connection to one woman passing, then turned as she passed, with both of us smiling. A seagull emerged where light mist met water. The city seemed distant marble.

I slipped, then sort of skied on one leg and landed on my butt. North Meadow Tennis Center looked appealing. As I approached the fence I fell again, straining my wrists this time. I hadn't reached out for the tennis-court fence. White knots hung where wires crossed. The furthest courts already had nets.

Climbing home I moved as naturalistically as possible before one woman poised with a camera. She winced and waited for me to pass. Nobody had descended the marble staircase to The Meer. Today was full of privileges. A string of Christo's Gates still arced around the cove. Volunteers shared shoveling. Everyone seemed thrilled. Geese and ducks lined the bank with buried faces. I couldn't stop looking into a South American woman's eyes but the whole time I wondered Why do I look at people?

A Nordic couple programmed their camera, posed beneath a gate bearing ruddy infants. An Irish woman hailed a dog walker, passed a disposable camera, propped herself beside red ladders hung along The Meer. Did you have a white Christmas? the Irish woman asked. The annoyed photographer reined in his cairn which had fully stretched its flexi-leash.

On the final turn I followed a black man from the neighborhood (also with camera). We both stayed relaxed and emotionally present. There ought to be a language for this.

WEDNESDAY

The Taiwanese girl overtook me in Kristin's lobby, spinning to say goodbye to Raphael, sprinting towards the revolving door still tugging on her mom's sleeve. The mother flashed a glittering Barbie bag. My face felt flush at 9:05. Gray sky hung pretty bright in patches.

Parents stood talking in Parkschool Daycare. Most had on expensive jeans. A stencil read The United Rubber Company: If it's made with rubber we have it. A sign's font—DESIGNER'S CHOICE—somehow indicated trashy clothing. Neither place exists anymore. Deliverymen shoved stacked boxes into a ten dollar or less boutique for women. A pudgy cashier watched from his window. I partially wanted to sit beside him. Light fixtures had been painted to resemble trees.

A diagram praised the Woolworth Building. A rope read No Tourists Beyond This Point. St. Paul's (oldest active church in the country) stood chained. Its dim panel displayed George Washington's pew.

Temp workers passed promos out on Broadway: free newspapers and cellphone plans. One woman really put her heart in it; Good morning guys! Take a look! Between greetings she mumbled negative thoughts.

Both entrances to a lingerie shop showed lines of dozens of brass female legs—I assume this place is famous. A young corporate couple flinched as a guy in camouflage pressed You've *never* been there? A cop directing traffic around a bus gauged this situation from across the street.

By Trinity Church I got sick of display panels. In the cemetery the snow stayed white. The most sunken slabs were entirely covered. The ancient urban hues reminded me of pigeons. "Tuppence a Bag" stuck in my head. Reflections made it hard to read but almost everyone seemed to have died around forty, with kids who died their first year (spelled firft). Several stones lay completely bare. From the side-exit subway commuters cut a path (or am I condensing memories: at some point, underground, I passed the side-entrance to a sports bar called Suspenders; a sign said Bathroom For Customers Only; a tall woman's stilettos never touched one step as we all crammed upwards then burst into day). Four young men praised their boss's bottom line. Trinity Place's footbridge sat locked.

I snaked through office towers just to see which guards would stop me. The lamplight was rich and non-fluorescent. Elevators chimed decorated with charming grids. On Pine I scanned a large display of business shoes. I couldn't help comparing models and prices. The letters N-e-w Y-o-r-k U-n-i-v-e-r-s-i-t-y S-c-h-o-o-l o-f M-a-n-a-g-e-m-e-n-t had been stripped from the building but left a permanent stain. I paused above an alley of external escalators. It seemed I'd sleptwalked there one summer.

A block to the north loomed a burned looking cross. Foreign tourists filled the Trade Center site. The city had mounted sepia-tinted photos of Lower Manhattan's skyline circa 1914. The model for Calvatrava's subway station looked just like his Milwaukee Art Museum. The destroyed area appeared, as it always does, huge and very compact.

I turned on Vessey which turned into Ann St., where a delivery truck split the sidewalk. I followed Williams and curved through loggias. I passed my old job at 59 Maiden Lane. The same fruit guy hit on customers.

Signs for cheap restaurants made it hard to look around. Shellacked burritos spread across checked tables. Soon I'd entered the Woolworth Building, feeling flushed and glittery. There are even grander spaces further inside I thought. When I got to the guard I asked if she gave tours during business hours. I asked about weekends, then explained I'm a professor at a local college and want to bring students for an official tour. I spun amid the churchy glow. On the way out a no-entry sign read Witkoff Management—what shitheads.

Afterwards I stopped in Bellbates for bananas, mangoes, brown rice. Passing Raphael I realized I didn't have keys. Still I rode up to Kristin's then rode back down, so when I asked for the spare it seemed natural.

THURSDAY

Steps stood blowsy with scraps at 8:26. How do tabloid sheets get torn into triangles? How does wind ball plastic bags so tightly? The few clouds came as trails from airplanes. Sled tracks seemed made of styrofoam. One man concentrated coasting through the park. His thick bike looked expensive. He was beaming and had a beard—a scientist maybe. My own mind filled with calculations.

I kept pushing the walk button at Central Park West. Wind opened tiny cuts in my face. When I had the chance I crossed through scaffolds where trash hovered, spiraling. Grocery carts rusted locked to one deli. Latino men squatted against a computer store. A smiling Arab dad tossed them keys. Nearby bikes had missing parts. Wheelless and seatless bike frames sprawled on their backs like tortured horses. I felt extra focused walking along a fence.

Now that Columbia kicked out the West Side Market a new Garden of Eden had gone in on Broadway. I didn't know how to feel about it. An African worker wearing kneepads bore himself with dignity. A drunk white guy leered at a Tibetan family. Wet appliance boxes lined the curb. Printouts posted to bus-stop awnings advertised violin lessons. Plastic protecting deli produce hung held down with ice buckets.

As police entered Commerce Bank the lobby let out canned accordion tunes. A bare construction light-bulb left me seeing purple. The primary colors along Symphony Space helped calm me down. The lone adult with head uncovered cheerfully hailed a cab. Within a still-darkened beauty salon somebody talking on his cellphone shivered.

A woman's Kosher Market bags inspired my turn east. I looked enthusiastically for the place but never stopped and searched. I wondered why certain puddles hadn't frozen. Amid bright patches nestled near delis today felt bodiless like dust. A Puerto Rican nurse informed her shih tzu: Look I'm already taking extra minutes, since they owe me, but you *gotta* get moving. The dog stared without an expressive face.

In front of laundromat mirrors a woman buttoned her blazer. A slender woman fumbled through a purse directly opposite a porcelain Virgin Mary. Of another woman all I saw was the tattoo of skeleton wings (from Colonial tombstones) right above her butt. The back of her shirt drooped as she bent to clear a van with its side-door open. I paused to read the ingredients list on a five-gallon drum of salad dressing. This almost caused a collision with a different woman (annoyed). Across Amsterdam a pile of moldering newspapers and ice dissolved into nothing. I guess it becomes the air we breathe. A Brazilian kickboxing dojo kept up last fall's voter-registration drive. A Cuban restaurant smelled good but I felt bourgeois gawking at its menu.

Back at 109th four men gathered near the hill's steepest point. They speculated on an upcoming boxing match. The speaker sounded embarrassed to use the word technique. A gray-haired man—grinning, laptop in his leather bag—jogged with body torqued to read the number on a bus. It passed. He slowed to the urgent walk that ends up damaging your shins.

At Lenox a frantic white woman almost hit several Latino moms. She honked towards a black businessman in a hurry. A separate person screamed as two guys ducked behind scaffolds. Don't you come round my place, she warned. I got 12 small kids. The woman looked 55, the men around 30. One popped out as if to confront her, just giggled. Then back in the courtyard the stairs had been swept.

FRIDAY

Beyond the lobby glass it looked freezing. I almost couldn't go. But the temperature was normal at 9:06. My bowels felt caramelized. A flyer offered one-bedrooms for $1850. A woman scrawled in curly writing Harlem? Are you fucking crazy? A grandma shouted greetings, sounded healthy. A tall policeman outside a bodega reminded me of its door.

Crossing into light I turned up Adam Clayton Powell. Someone with pants tucked in his boots staggered down the sidewalk. When I bent to flip a notecard he veered at me snarling. For the next couple blocks I wouldn't look at anybody. Shy like that I could barely see the ground. I thought about a seminar paper I wrote long ago, how its title should have been Eye Contact. The proximity of parks made where I stood suffocating. Abruptly I curved off to St. Nick's Ave. I was wrong: it's not the street I like, that's Convent. Soon there weren't pedestrians, just signs for condos. A car's top held citations from Corinthians (just numbers). A limping white pigeon had skin disease.

St. Nick's Park appeared under sky I think looked so blue because of the hill's angle. The staircase I climbed cast zigzag shadows. Instincts led through City College campus right to Cohen Library. A guard I talked to winced at questions. A Serbian couple wore swishy athletic suits. The boy tried to pry our elevator open. The girl had such a charming face. When they got off one flight up I continued ascending with somebody meek but can't really remember this.

The circulation guy forgot to scan *Cameraworks*, but I headed through sensors anyway. I liked the Bangladeshi clerk for his threadbare cardigan and slender fingers. An alarm went off. I rolled my eyes. Both escalators dropped beneath giant photographs of young black people perched in windows—the '69 student takeover. TV monitors produced a drowning sensation. Back on Convent I gave myself a pep talk (aloud) about how silly it is to think the same thought twice. I saw Ward's Island Bridge arcing west toward Spanish Harlem. A woman climbed a ramp in an electric cart. She joked with whoever had held the door, cruised off with a curve that seemed to say See you later.

Fenced pits lay abandoned at 129th. Trash floated (mostly 16-ounce bottles). Two police cars honked as if I hadn't seen them coming. I blinked and kicked some ice which ended up being thick crystal glass. I was having a moment where my hands feel unbearably hot inside gloves.

At 118th a black girl in mauve got so transfixed by a flabby construction guy's stare. A svelte woman stepped down from a church. I felt like a creep for checking her out. She'd probably attended a funeral unless this was Easter weekend or somehow Easter related. Men above spoke kindly but to me they were a wall.

Ragtime drifted through a windowpane. A shy boy asked if the key-cutting store was open yet. The shaved bald clerk replied We're *open* open. Women with Watchtowers sensed I wasn't interested. Both faces slackened.

Central Park stood white and blank. It's strange no one lives in the building next to ours. In the hall Luis and Frankie pushed refrigerators. I slunk past before they could pause in the extra inch my doorway provides.

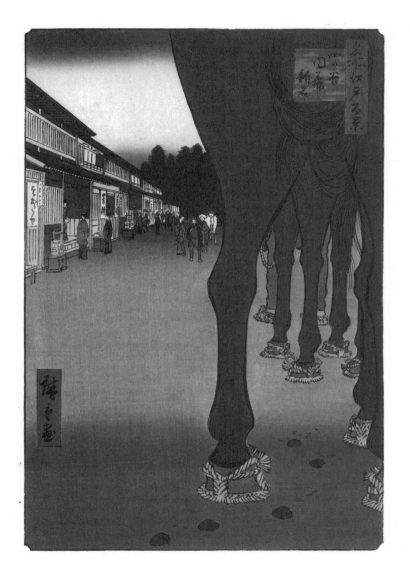

...then broke ranks as they passed smeared horse poop clumps.

MONDAY

Still spinning out Kristin's door I decided to change plans.
The air stirred gently, made me think of flags. At 9:26 I saw
the clean white backs of waitresses in a Gee Whiz Diner
window.

Someone in charcoal suit and tie sprinted across
Chambers toward a pharmacy. It hadn't opened. He turned
back to his car. I took off my coat and bunched it. I crossed
between busses, blinking when a photo of fast-food chicken
got in my face, cutting east with a blind woman and her
father. A kid weaving a handcart through everyone wore a
baseball hat that said *Caire*ful.

Tribeca smelled like soft rolls and coffee. Office
towers from the seventies stood tinted pleasant green. All
the scaffolds dripped on Broadway. Squares had been torn
to let a sapling through. A bush on Franklin held a plump
melodic sparrow. A woman smiling at someone behind me
waved in case I'd misunderstood. I turned up White but
can't remember it. I don't remember Church except for
the clapping sound of pigeons' wings. At Canal I dropped
into the art-deco post office thinking Union Station L.A. I
asked a clerk where to find passport applications.

Monday no passport she said, never glancing up.
Tuesday Saturday Window 20. Monday Window 20 closed.

Near the exit I passed Window 20. To me it appeared
open. From Thompson I remembered dreaming about fire
escapes last night. I felt at ease across from six-story columns
identified as Shaftways. A parking attendant dragged his
chair into the center of the sun. He closed his eyes but kept
talking to the co-worker behind him.

A street sweeping truck followed me down Spring.
This scared a floppy spaniel which nonetheless kept up its

owner's brisk pace. Two blonds seemed thrilled to be tall and heading to work and more generally everyone looked buoyant. The joy hinted that it would last. Handsome black men took off helmets, walked motor scooters along the curb. My big toe ached from pushing too hard. I stuffed my hat in a coat pocket.

Damp air blowing in from Chinatown smelled like mushroom bulk bins. There were so many 50-pound bags of onions. There were ashy carrots as thick as forearms. I couldn't pause to examine fish but I did appreciate bubbling tanks. I split through murmuring couples. Hunched women stopped to consider produce. Others turned so gradually I saw it coming a hundred feet off. Someone Haitian called out Cel-e-*ry* to his grinning Chinese counterpart—an old guy in appealing thin pants. Behind them somebody mentally-retarded passed by unattended, wiggled her foot, pushed beyond the disjointed blocks between Bayard and Confucius Plaza.

One Asian girl in gold tights and sneakers helped an ancient couple cross Catherine. Upon close inspection all three looked gray.

I got to Chatham Square Library just as it opened. The clerk fixated on a tower of DVD check-ins before retrieving my John Cage audio hold. The neighborhood grew steamy. Someone catching crates of strawberries couldn't help squishing each box he caught. Somebody paced herself to pass between boxes. A woman sidled up to a police officer and asked without eye contact Where's the World Trade?

As we waited out the light one mom started blinking. Her non-glossy freckled skin reminded me of cookies. Soon we were smiling, mostly staring straight ahead. Saturated with goodwill I strode right toward my favorite Bellbates cashier before even grabbing a handcart.

Back at Church a girl's wheelchair glistened. A cook drenched the sidewalk with soapy water. In Park Dayschool it was story time. The woman had gray dreadlocks.

TUESDAY

No one had an umbrella so I assumed it wasn't raining. But from the door I saw drops slap a white garbage bag. By 7:30 pools gathered in its creases.

With snow gone I wanted to check out the Conservatory Gardens. Ducks paddled stoically across The Meer. Swans didn't look distinct yet. Seagulls' feet get so much yellower here than Battery Park. Three women hoisting umbrellas came toward me in a solid line, taking up the entire walk, then broke ranks as they passed smeared horse poop clumps. A wide green garbage truck passed next—I had to spin sideways to let it fit. There was something Japanese about the wobbly boots park workers wore as they speared paper scraps in the rain. The chords geese behind us honked tingled like seltzer.

Chains circled the Gardens. I'd come too early. Plants seemed somehow put away. Where I crossed 5th a cab almost crushed a girl. She stayed quiet about it. I screamed Idiot through the passenger's window. Through a basement window on E. 102nd I watched great quantities of sandwiches and some mayonnaise-soaked side dish get wrapped. Loosely chopped lettuce heads spilled down a long counter/cutting board. Tins of sliced tomatoes lined up red and filled with seeds.

Black school children waited for busses, too many to fit under the fiberglass. At the crowd's edge a blond stroked his tense sons' bangs. Are you sure you're OK? he said. You look silly.

Coming out from Long Island Railroad tracks I found a bed-table wallpapered blue with white stars. I turned amid cops in orange rainproof headdress (a straggler jogged behind, chubby and really bending his knees).

On the walk up Lexington it became clear that pedestrians with no umbrellas moved non-committally while people under cover set a quick pace. Between Kim's Nails and Our Laundry sprawling, frustrated groups waited for several busses. A Poland Springs water bottle sailed down the curb. Tough guys clasped hands without ever speaking. One crowded store sold cakes and balloons. A mural for Popate (1973-1994) included a cross-eyed man's portrait, a Puerto Rican flag, a moonlit inscription: From Family And Friends.

As I continued north a contact lens began to flutter. I kept having to stare to dissipate the film. People weren't comfortable with this but the alternate option was to wink a lot. I knew I'd been approaching the Triborough Bridge but couldn't remember how it connects to the Bronx. Geographically I'd grown confused; it felt like someone might jump me. At 131st, where Lexington ends, a giant Sanitation warehouse starts. Oldies songs drift at modest volumes. Hot twin clerks in an office supply store called out from distant display-room desks.

On the way down Madison my knees began to fade. The evening before I'd biked Manhattan twice. Passing the Mt. Morris Turkish Baths (underground at the corner, like any innocuous subway stop) I wondered if they could still possibly exist. The gate blew open, actually. A girl protected by a vinyl rain cap frowned just beyond her mother's umbrella.

Sloshing across Marcus Garvey Park I pushed up stairs with waning strides. At the peak a timid white person approached asking me to sell him a cigarette. Temporarily stunned, I said No thanks. The spiraling tower at the park's tip stood locked. Still there was a pleasing amount of space. The swimming pool lay filled with muck. Through branches Fifth Avenue resembled strips of stars.

The park path dropped me south, which seemed fine, though I'd grown self-conscious about the broken zipper on the khakis I always wear in the rain. A muscular guy's miniature collie yapped at cars but always managed to heel. On 116th a Harlem Sports Club's Coming Soon window-display looked pretty disorganized. On 112th a co-op's multiple doormen suggested high-security gentrification was already well in progress.

On 111th city workers strained to unhook a manhole cover. I'd always wondered if these are heavy. When I paid for orange juice at the nearest bodega a kid asked Y'all got headphones? This stayed inscrutable as I passed through the lobby provisioned and spent.

WEDNESDAY

Kristin came from the elevator, which smelled like coffee. The florist had installed yellow daisies, yellow lilies. At 8:12 I flinched against a frigid gust—couldn't get my lips wedged under a scarf. People's eyes expressed abandonment. I cancelled my walk along the Hudson and scurried toward the island's center. A suitcase held down someone's burrito-wrapped blanket. In the next alcove somebody mumbled reading tabloids atop a milk crate.

Judging from body language boys with facemasks were the coldest. For a block it turned too bright to look past sidewalk. A young malamute lay calmly breathing. Ethereal X's ran up a building façade (these seemed maybe to come from hubcaps). Broadway had been so heavily salted I couldn't gauge how much snow there was. Under Leonard Street scaffolds ice-dust glimmered. A white man slipped then ended up doing the splits near City Hall. A Korean couple in high-tech winter gear spoke intimately, moved gracefully. A bareheaded cop guarding the state courthouse smiled; he appeared just to have remembered something.

Columbus Park had been eviscerated. Pipes lay everywhere. Trucks' blond shovels hung filled with snow. Along a hastily assembled fence I slipped and strained my neck catching balance. Along Baxter Chinese women talked and did aerobics. One's hips wouldn't stop shimmying. I spun off in vicarious ecstasy.

I couldn't feel the cold as a laughing girl crossed Canal in clogs and yellow neon socks. Behind her men pushed delivery carts: four Andyboy lettuce boxes, four marked TROUT. There weren't any Italians yet on Mulberry. They must all drive in from out of state. One dark-skinned boy chipped away at ice. One door sat surrounded by olive oil tins. The one gay pride flag for blocks had gotten entangled in fire escape steps. Neatly stacked Malaysian newspapers stood bound and stamped Recycling.

Pigeons spread up the sidewalk on Grand, tearing at cinnamon-raisin bagels. I plowed through then felt bad approaching their patron—a compact lady with bags. One mom strained to tie garbage bags without taking off gloves. One squat guy hauled heavy cement-mix bags to a pick-up. Each time he spun back to the vestibule he faced chic tall mannequins in short denim skirts. He seemed to appreciate this.

A woman knelt wrapped in verdant shades I'd never seen anybody wear. After we glanced in each other's eyes I looked at flower barrels, a parking garage. Mulberry ended at Lafayette, where someone had written across the bus-stop sign Except there is no such bus on weekends! I walked on subway grates since these felt the least icy. I love any enfolding path of gridded metal squares. I got excited watching a restaurant's cellar door rise. It turned out to be a mechanized process.

Cancun Lounge (adjacent to Woo Lae Oak, my first job in New York) had been converted into a fish bar with an abstract one-word title. The big design change was slightly more neutral tones. A drop of water fell in my mouth as I passed the store for kid geniuses. A resident's recycling bin overflowed with green bottles. Latino contractors huddled in lobbies, except one woman washed windows in just a teal sweatshirt. Someone carrying a load of bricks spaced out, screamed Sorry, crashed into me. Crossing Canal I could barely ignore movie billboards where the tunnel dropped. I straightened as an attractive waitress passed and our faces seemed bizarrely close.

I got confused at the diagonal intersection with Varick and ended up sprinting across in a panic though it turned out I had a walk sign. Tree-branch shadows flickered off busses. Otherwise they didn't exist. A potted fir tipped in front of the expensive French restaurant on Duane. A couple windows flashed open in the Cosmopolitan Hotel. Those rooms must have been unbearably hot. On my way back to the elevator, as I passed Raphael, "Hello" never got through my rigid jaws—my lips just moved silently.

THURSDAY

Luis was talking with an older resident when I stepped out of the stairwell. I knew he wanted to remind me of the exterminators coming. I slid brusquely through the arch their bodies made. At 8:17 cold air stayed still.

I crossed through scaffolds strung with caged lamps. Icicles and nails poked down near the exit. Silence and light gathered around tabloid salesmen seated on milk crates at 110th and Lenox. Slashed garbage bags spilled their contents. Shredded documents clung to each other. Books sprawled, some flapping. The guy ahead grabbed several without slowing down. There was a Benito Cellini, P.G. Wodehouse, Kathy Acker. There were also hundreds of greeting cards.

Curled shoots like thin green tongues kept unbinding themselves in sidewalk plots. I crouched to read a plant's identification tag. Dark ice showed where bus passengers spilled coffee. Across the street joggers expelled mist onto shrubs: a different morning.

A girl chipped ice off an SUV. She used something small like a credit card, looked 80% hypnotized. A Vermont Bus Lines coach turned south though its destination board read Bangor. An old Jamaican dropped his walkman—scattering silver plastic. He flinched then spun around before stooping to pick things up. After carrying home too many books last night I could barely peek in the farmers' market. My neck and back muscles wouldn't bend. Spasms flickered like lightning bolts somewhere around my kidneys. A dwarf carried her mesh Speedo bag off one shoulder (two bananas inside).

An elderly pedestrian adjusted a yarmulke. His torso stayed bent perpendicular to his legs. The steepest part of this stretch sat covered in paper cups and pieces of rolls from subway platforms. People are always tossing out rolls. Staring toward a departed 9 train felt like almost remembering something. Boy Scouts distributed carwash flyers. At 125th I turned east.

A blond Latino woman cradled a child wrapped in pastel blankets, even its face. Amid blue sky and snow someone winding down the path from a General Grant Housing Project caught my attention. He looked at home here. The restrictive internal cramps I used to get around housing projects were gone. This happened across from a place called El Tina. A man murmured Cigarettes. Cigarettes. Cigarettes.

A crumbling marquee read Welcome to Harlem, U.S.A. At the corner someone slowed, muttered Marlboros...Newports. Copy machines rusted under traffic lights. Vendors laid blankets on plywood tables. The crossing guard beside me blew her whistle. Both thighs began chafing against my jeans.

(Just as expected) it became hard to walk one of Manhattan's main east-west thoroughfares without mostly losing consciousness. One girl's backpack was a yarn head with dreadlocks.

Cutting through Marcus Garvey Park I recognized the hysterical collie from Tuesday's walk. This dog sprinted in diminishing circles. Its master kept handing himself the leash overhead. Snow caught in masonite reminded me of etchings. A pit bull wore an expensive red top. Pale boys shied along the fence and stared at the owner. She seemed happy with that.

Back on my own block I studied birdhouses nestled within a gingko. A bulbous sparrow peeked out from one. A businesswoman ate a big doughnut for breakfast. I ended up liking today.

FRIDAY

I stepped out at 9:02 in Boston, in Jamaica Plain, in glasses. Like a drug addict I'd forgot to bring contact solution or even a case. Sidewalks only had snaky paths shoveled. Pizza boxes filled blue recycling bins. Breeze smelled wintry before and after one short man's cigar.

A waitress nodded out El Oriental De Cuba's door like she'd just reached a big decision. Bottles scattered along the curb pointed away from each other, which seemed somehow festive. Tufts of pine needles made every sidewalk square unique. I stood half-sunken, hoping to cross Jamaica Way, whining that cars never would stop.

As I approached the pond two joggers caught up from behind. One unleashed his lab just to calm it down. A black poodle appeared—guarded at first. Then it showed with every conceivable gesture that it wanted to be chased.

There were dog tracks crisscrossing Jamaica Pond's ice. Dogs would lead then trail their masters. Geese crouched off a grassy island. I'd forgotten how emotional I get around crows.

Keys hung from a bush on Eliot Street. Shovels stood (vertically) in the middle of someone's yard. I didn't want to pass another auto-parts place. From the opposite direction poked a war monument. Inside Harvest Co-op a nun pointed at the freezer. Lactaid free rice milk ice cream she said. I labeled bulk goods with Whitney Houston singing "Saving All My Love for You" in the background, feeling ok. But the next song was so bad I started talking to myself in the bread aisle.

Scott and Jessica's felt far as soon as I'd bought groceries. Passers-by surrendered sidewalk so our bags wouldn't touch. White cars looked dirty against fresh snow. A gas station's flags flapped dull and salty. I convinced myself I'd missed a turn and now sat lost with heavy bundles. Postal activities had been transferred to a shed while the elegant main building got repaired. I identified with workers. My eyes were streaming.

Inside CVS it felt so sterile and continuous I considered stealing saline just to ground myself. Instead my bags toppled lotion boxes. A fun employee said Don't worry, it's a trick.

Where I curved around a pick-up a builder told his boss I'm fifty years old but still nothing: I don't have a *house*; I don't have a *cah*. Recycling bins blew across Paul Gore (reminding me of the moonwalk). A mom assumed I would sprint in front of her and honked. As so often happens with guest keys mine got stuck. Desperate for a bathroom I whirled and yanked.

A cherry tree's crooked branches suggested a thousand elbows.

MONDAY

With cars honking on the way downstairs I could have been outside. Frankie swept the front hall at 8:06. OK! he said. A young Vietnamese family made Lenox glow. I didn't put on a hat until I'd mailed postcards to my grandparents. I approached the park with a brochure in my pocket, pledging to find The Ravine.

Four tall geese patrolled the western Meer. Ripples and floating scraps glistened. A hockey stick poked from the garbage and the lettering on it pleased me. The rink seemed hard to face unless you liked corporate logos. The only snow left lay in shoveled piles. Fallen leaves looked shiny but weren't at all wet.

Under Huddlestone Arch appeared crates stuffed with a homeless person's things: shoes and maybe an abacus. The tile-ceiling tunnel felt tight. Pants dried draped along waterfall rocks.

Climbing out from The Ravine I wanted to cross through fields. Even baseball diamonds were blocked. A sign slated them to open mid-April. As I scanned North Meadow my mind rehearsed an argument I'll probably get in this afternoon. A cherry tree's crooked branches suggested a thousand elbows. Benches glimmered. Frozen salted patches dried pink.

Shepherds surrounded an unleashed setter named Liza, sniffing until she strayed beyond their circumference. Nice moves! Liza's owners cried as she paused where the path curved. We dropped to the East Meadow with its hundred autonomous dogs. Some lay on benches with leashes in their mouths. Most sat stationary. Two rolled on top of each other while a rich boy mumbled commands. A woman's exquisitely patterned stockings got me thinking about the Weimar Republic. I climbed back towards E. 98th very much sensitive to depth and light.

My bright shadow on garden tiles confirmed the momentum of spring. A golf cart sat there with keys on the cushion. A blue jay shrieked then dove in a shrub. I was disappointed not to see any crocus shoots or snowdrops but later, calmer, I noticed that snowdrops and crocus bulbs surrounded me. Magnolia buds almost poked my eye. Someone smoked at the far end of an ivy-covered galley (is that even a word?). The sounds off a street sweeping truck made the scene more universal.

A Sunday Times Magazine drooped where branches stretched across Fifth. At the corner of 5th and 108th an attractive nurse stepped through a window, into what turned out to be a stuffy parlor. Somebody placed chairs at an attentive angle to traffic. One lady alternated reading tabloids and staring. Behind her others looked vacant.

On Lexington I spotted Jaguar Restaurant—what an exciting name. At 106th a glossy poster announced Latino townhall meetings. I wondered if anybody beyond the organizers would attend. Political optimism surged through me. An androgynous child sprinted past in a faded, leopard-print jacket. A cat slunk down the sidewalk. Will you follow I cried, swerving amid tremendous glass shards. The cat dove through a sewer grate. A rubble-strewn lot appeared empty but I sensed grackles rooting about. In an adjacent lot a State of New York truck idled, polluted, warmed thick men with a crossword.

Hidden by a rooftop ledge sparrows creaked like a wooden wheel. Trains sent pleasing vibes through the shadows. As one male pigeon chased a zigzagging female both pretended this wasn't happening. An African boy unwound the brightest scarf I'd ever seen. A teenager stood staring at the lobby. I tried not to notice. He followed me in.

TUESDAY

Luis stopped outside the stairwell to see which resident was coming. He recognized my shoes and passed on. I stepped out wrapped for winter at 8:36. The new Spanish graffiti along our trash bins didn't faze me. The Park Hotel (Lenox) had for once opened its café. The yellow-orange interior reminded me of Café Gitane (Mulberry). Two men sat apart wearing puffy coats. Nobody worked the tables.

I turned left three straight times since I'd never seen the back of my building. It still looked obscure. Across the street stretched a 50-yard-dash track barely contained by a sprawling fence (so that you'd have to crash or slow down early). The bald, gold-skinned guy walked his daughter to school. They didn't touch but shared an electric bond. One bus displayed milk packaged in many different volumes.

Continuing north between Robert Taft homes ripped-up bagels remained a constant. I sensed City Choir symbols suggested goodness. They also resembled a police badge. (Like always) one mattress had been tossed out. Somebody I'd never expect to talk to fixed his stare from a long way off. What's your price? he finally said. I turned past giant flowerpots painted to resemble Puerto Rican flags. A dead rat lay with its snout piercing a deli roll (looking cute like that). Most storefronts seemed abandoned campaign offices for City Council or State Assembly.

Further down 116th, on my way past a prominent A.M.E. church, the song "Iron, Lion, Zion" lingered in my head. When an ambulance passed I didn't plug my ears, out of respect for the neighborhood. Reflections off commuter trains made Barrio Electronics pulse. This lasted longer than expected and left me mystical. Bright Mexican flags swelled strung from streetlamps. White people reappeared like flurries.

A woman approached as I watched clouds: Do you have change for a dollar? Sorry, I said, like she was a beggar. Her plastic bag had started to rip where the detergent box poked through. Whenever I moved in front my butt tightened. Whenever she passed I watched her hips rock. Wondering if our bodies were saying the same thing I glanced down into a garden-level bakery where the breads looked crusty and real.

116th soon became a footbridge. Dog poop somehow lined the handrails. The river's green dimples resembled cosines. On my return across the bridge, as I watched a stout man fold where the highway kinked, it gradually grew clear he wasn't stretching but was gesturing lewdly, following crotch thrusts by wiggling a racket between his legs. A police car passed. Rolls of fat peeked out. Drivers honked benevolent rhythms.

I hit Pleasant Avenue—which I'd never heard of, and which seemed to end with the Robert Wagner Homes. It was boring how many businesses put Pleasant in their titles. A park fence curled back so that kids could enter standing. A flyer offered between $100 and $1,000,000 for the return of a greyhound. Another concerned a missing elderly man: frowning, looking Dominican.

114th felt overwhelmingly Catholic. Two women hailing cabs made the street smell like hairspray. There was some sort of National Catholic Center, a charitable thrift shop, a cylindrical Health Services building from which a Puerto Rican grandmother stepped, smoking as she pushed a carriage (with Keds and chapped teenage-girl shins). Tan Timberland baby boots hung inside consecutive cars. A string of garbage bags held tiny rat holes at their bottoms. A squirrel leapt from one mouthing wadded toilet paper. Black mannequins in beige miniskirts stared down from a fourth-floor balcony.

When I reached 110th I found the milk truck from before, closed now but idling as its driver read a tabloid. Dixie cups stood stacked where loose barbed wire sagged. A purple zebra could be ridden for a quarter. One New York State employee swept my block with a broom. One girl stopped to ask if I had 15 cent. When I explained (truthfully) I've got nothing, she replied Shit! (more emotional than expected).

WEDNESDAY

Women passed the lobby with their hands in sleeves. But it felt mild for 8:56. I wore my grandpa's windbreaker and just held my gloves. A teenager gnawed an unlit cigar. A pasty professional grabbed his Thai girlfriend at the top of the 2-3 steps. Flower islands sat full of fresh dirt. Plaza traffic flowed north-south.

On 112th a calm Indian man hosed stairs, curbside garden plots, a gleaming SUV. Spiraling barbed-wire split the roofs. A woman slowed ahead, intrigued by something in her paper. A stoop sign read No Standing/ " Sitting/ " Hopscotch while across the street one stated No Sitting/ No Music/ No Ball Playing/ No Standing. As a super kicked a loveseat past he glanced up imploringly. Cardboard boxes lay strung with orange twine.

Further west hung a sign for Always Organic. I'd never seen this store. I checked its hours. A Japanese girl covered her teeth and laughed in a payphone. A black man also looked vulnerable—pausing on the staircase in his Pittsburgh Steelers jacket.

As I cut across Morningside Park's baseball diamond each step broke cold dirt clumps into soil. With my puffy shoe-heel I kicked a baseball twice. I was worried it might still be frozen at the center. Shredded paper floated on the pond. A well-trained mutt fought off chasing robins.

Halfway up the stairs daffodils unfurled. A coffee scent intensified. A lot of Riverside Park's benches had been removed. Only stone legs remained. Approaching the Hudson I put on my hat. Across the river four identical buildings trailed off to the horizon (New Jersey). A dog owner peeked in a maintenance truck. There's a bag on the trail, the guy said, That um looks like a body.

Where I continued north two women joggers deeply engaged in conversation curved. Above Grant's Tomb hung a flag I'm not familiar with: white dots on vermillion, perhaps Tennessee. Police barricades lined Passive Lawn. I forget the Japanese name of the park this was in (starts with a K). I've always found it promising.

Straying towards the Manhattan School of Music my face stirred with sun for the first time this spring. I wondered if circles under a Sikh security guard's eyes necessarily meant he was tired. I couldn't get around a cute angry person with this knitted purple wrap on her head. We just mirrored each other's motion, like in volleyball drills. Shadows played across posted signs. I was glad they were there. I'd never known Morningside Park was so long. From the bottom step rose a shin-high pyramid of toxic seeming pink crystals. I hurried past without inhaling, crossed cement tagged Young Guns of 117th, came upon a diamond-eyed, close-cropped boy earnestly walking a dog for his father.

On 116th, under Arabic awnings, I appreciated that Muslims emphasize green. African restaurants held fun names, like Slow Down. A taxi had been parallel parked along the curb; I pictured someone driving it home. I passed a post office I might use sometime. A strapped-in baby's head bobbed as the mother moved gently to catch a bus. People paused to smile at this. Somebody stood and said Do you have even a quarter? He had to hold one lens from his glasses in place. Staff fanned out from a funeral parlor. Sledgehammers started so I turned south.

Banners on a derelict mosque celebrated some program called City Lives. Men wearing facemasks dropped debris in the dumpster. A flyer warned Harlem Residents: Your city plans to raise property taxes 200% on June 25th. A woman pushed against a disreputable church.

Inside a boarded-up deli detergent boxes went blank. A grackle picked at buffalo wings. This bird stopped and met my stare from the sidewalk. There were flattened wads of gum all around.

THURSDAY

I spun out from Kristin's at 8:14 against the enlivening gravelly air. Business people passed by harried and alone. Cement trucks corkscrewed past. Across Greenwich a woman exiting a cab clenched her butt. She was into herself and wore all white.

Around Harrison dusty workers smoked beneath a giant blue Putzmeister crane. Why do fenced-off construction sites make me feel small, lonely and connected to the world? Skyscrapers along the New Jersey coast all looked the same color as my personal checks. One storefront rivaled Milton's description of Chaos. Placards put Jesus in blindfold next to a blind, grinning Mao. Only after a cart filled with recyclables had passed did I realize how oblivious I'd been of its presence. Pomeranians slowed to stare at poodles across the street.

Crowds converged on Citicorp's building as if by gravitational pull. A boy squatting with a laptop smiled (which completely hid his lips). Crossing Canal, listening to a couple murmur inside one car, it felt like I was still sleeping. Ahead of me an architect explained that what people call her quirky designs are just attempts to avoid all this lifelessness. Somebody blind scanned the intersection with his cane. Fingers peeked from a homeless person's quilt. Behind this someone else lay covered. The fresh morning smell had changed to damp boots.

I gazed into the dusty stillness of a sedan's rear dashboard and then there was a bible there. I passed a UPS warehouse in which you could just make out the workers' breaths. West African security guards joked with shippers, who stayed slightly more serious. Nothing rode on the conveyor belts. All of this repeated itself for blocks: 136 parking spaces. Afterwards Fed Ex began which somehow seemed less interesting.

From Perry a jogger passed in shorts and I remembered I'd soon see a lot of flesh in public. Kids grouped around a crossing guard might have all been models. Preoccupied women strode past in leather pants. Two bags of piss leaned against a tree. Two rotund men in shades wore their blue and white headdress like Yasser Arafat's. Everybody else paused walking a dog. A basset pup wouldn't sniff a magnolia, no matter how aggressive its owner's commands.

Crossing Jane I looked just as a mother yawned—I felt a part of this. A dad and son drank blue Elixir concoctions through straws. Amid bobbing tulips I saw that Congress opened Alaska for 24 billion barrels of oil. At Taylor's Bakery blond women sipped chai as their daughters sampled rice-krispie squares.

Shimmering lawns surrounded St. Luke in the Fields, restored my faith in the variety of birds. I got lost remembering songs by The Smiths. A sophisticated Southern woman held up a coffee-stand line asking why she'd only been charged a dollar fifty. A prep cook shielded his gold-toothed smile. Construction guys turned to watch a redhead pass. The shortest carried bags of gears on his shoulder. As I crossed he said Except she'd only be wearing ski boots.

In an alcove on Jay a cop and his daughter shared a chocolate doughnut with pink sprinkles. A knife knocked chicken cubes along a deli counter. I stepped through scattered proof pages chopped in thirds. My biggest criticism of nurses, one read, is that they often treat the patient to fit the pattern. Your nurse thinks, "I've got four patients to bathe before coffee break." The feeling she communicates is, "You're going to brush your teeth whether you like it or not." I flipped the scrap over: After I returned home from the hospital that winter [1978], I would crawl up stairs on my hands and knees. I was too unsteady to walk.

Without conscious effort I turned west on Duane, avoided the TV mounted at Chambers. Brothers did push-ups along the pavement with someone about sixty smiling above them. An onion stood against a scooter wheel beside the entrance steps to Salaam Bombay. The garbage bins overflowed with nan.

An old man on a treadmill wore headphones, cotton slacks, wingtips. I wondered how it felt to wear one woman's heels. Across from Baluchi's somebody told her boyfriend All this shit happened be*fore* your ass. Everything reflected off nearby windows, where waiters dished out chutneys.

FRIDAY

Fearing bronchitis I slept through the alarm and didn't get out until 9:15. From the courtyard sparrows whistled on either side. The day felt complete, a little tiring even. A police officer propped against a red door frowned when my glance made him self-conscious. It turns out the building east of mine's a corrections facility. I'd always thought it was a school.

Sudsy water along the curb made Fifth Ave. expansive and sensual. Bedrooms projected a broadcaster's voice. I can't remember crossing commuter tracks. Along the James Weldon Johnson Homes a black woman pointed at a white man's chest: You should have attended the *meet*ing I assigned! Audiocassette tape dangled from branches. Somebody called to a seventh-floor window I'm optimistic cause they said come back on Monday. Cars proclaimed themselves Trinidadian with red-and-white-striped everything. Sparrows guarding sliced wheat toast stayed surprisingly adept repulsing pigeons. A dirtbike abandoned next to boxes spun its wheels.

From 125th adults on train platforms seemed glamorous and made of vapor. Hmong carpenters assessed a storefront with all its wiring exposed. A woman with crutches propped herself to wait for the 101. Groups stood outside delis now that it was warm. The Bus Stop Kitchenette was packed: the diner-exhaust smell made me think of families.

Pink and beige balloons had become entwined to the back of a building called TRICHA 6. Within a block the streets turned barren. Spotting stuffed animals restored some inner strength. Both contact lenses began to flutter. When loud teens approached I stared ahead with a sense of purpose. A stream poured from one eye. I feigned wiping a nostril, just to somehow gesture, then lunged bizarrely towards them as they passed.

Behind dim Abraham Lincoln Homes a statue caressed a rising black boy's cheek. Cars veered around garbage bins wedged into potholes. Cigarettes lined the curb, McGeorge or something. A Peter Pan coach sped by en route to Boston and I remembered being sad to leave the city like this.

Where the Madison Avenue Bridge began a crushed grape jelly jar spread across pavement. I'd ascended out among tan projects. Industrial currents brought on a headache, made me feel like the product of furious whittling. I bent and found photographs of Bill Clinton. He looked angelic. An old guy in a Yankees cap biked around construction barrels. Demolished cars below had prices chalked across dashboards.

On the return trip to Manhattan I sensed that from one New York bridge you can always see others. A man slowed, saluted, said How you feeling chief? Wondering if Bronx people are extra friendly I made a Cuban jogger frown wishing her hello. My jacket pocket swelled and grazed a taut kid's thigh. A Puerto Rican grandfather peddled down Madison at just my pace. His bicycle gears creaked. The harmony with my mood and general worldview was exquisite. Beside women in wheelchairs waiting for busses a pale boy chewed on lottery printouts. A big white Italianate house's gingerbread drew me west. Someone around forty leaned from his van to engage twins dropping carpet at the curb. Two guys alternated squats on a Soloflex machine. They knew everybody.

The occasional white person crossing Lenox looked relieved to have me to fixate on. A drunken blonde in drag said Honey don't tell me you don't have a quarter. Rice covered sidewalk but there wasn't any church. An abandoned wheelchair blew against trash. A Jewish woman with a chihuahua in her bag asked if we were at all close to Columbus. The dog crouched (quiet and attentive).

Across 112th a Dominican man got lost imagining an argument. His voice kept coming as the distance grew between us. Beneath scaffolds I dodged dust clouds as debris hit dumpsters. By then it had to be about fifty degrees.

About twenty flew off, circled back…

MONDAY

At 8:04 I stepped out to find a damp chill freshness I associate with aviaries. In the patriotic deli on Murray St. union guys stood crammed. Latino contractors placed calls from a car with its doors wide open. The sneakers I was wearing had to constantly be retied. A mom looked distressed that I would enter an intersection hunched like this. Closed Irish taverns reinforced how I felt about today. Dark sidewalk lay filled with arrows, spray-painted numerals which told me nothing: 50-12.

Heading south on Church, on the way past a bank, I studied what clerks hung in cubicles (fewer photos than expected, more miniature stuffed basketballs). The person ahead spilled her groceries. A bottle bounced off the sidewalk without breaking, making an exquisite sound. When the woman bent her butt became a familiar icon into which I almost crashed.

I took Cedar just to cross beneath the giant Dubuffet. The stucco texture proved disappointing. Closer to it my senses stilled. Everything suddenly smelled like bacon.

From Pine I entered an indoor courtyard. Gray-haired men (all wearing green sweaters) stood in rectangles as if roped off. Homeless people occupied chairs along the periphery. Some outright slept but most just nodded amid spreads of newspapers, notebooks and bags.

Side doors led to Wall St. where I continued east or south, confused by wobbly Brooklyn Heights traffic floating beyond construction planks. Unfamiliar with certain tree barks I thought up identification plaques. Large wooden wheels had been laid along a pit. I wished they didn't have to all go underground. Just as I rushed to the East River docks a water-taxi pulled out for Weehawken—making everything vertiginous and sad. The Brooklyn and Manhattan Bridges looked good together. There was no birdshit-free space to rest my forearms. Water slurped against wood pylons.

Back on sidewalk I couldn't stop loving how a woman's suitcase wheels clicked every square. Strikers strode in front of several lobbies (bearing pamphlets but turned inwards). The Seaport Hotel was a particularly generic place I hope never to pass again. Businesses hung flags from windows. Barricades encircled the Stock Exchange. Guards steered pedestrians from surrounding blocks. Traders wearing badges drank coffee beside the guards. As I read about George Washington's first inauguration, at Federal Hall, somebody in a beret seemed to trip on a puddle.

A blond couple on Broadway passed a black man their camera. He grimaced as they positioned themselves. I wove away from busyness and ended up outside the Federal Reserve. Underneath, a plaque declared, lies a quarter of the world's gold bullion. But I couldn't tell which building. None was marked clearly. As I approached him a wiry adolescent inhaled like he wanted to say Hello. I said it. He didn't respond. A taxi door slammed, cars honked, drills thrust and pinged so that one tossed cigarette butt seemed so well-timed and colossal.

On Pearl a Haitian grandma scanned a gaudy display of business suits. On Fulton one guy's perfectly average haircut got me thinking about what a malignant force this (somehow truly innocent) city exerts upon the world (maybe all cities). I wondered why protests take place in parks, on weekends. Later a woman aimed a bullhorn at a fifth-floor office, accused its staff of kidnapping her son. You've *known* my name fifteen years, she cried. But never added it to your computers! You've already let me a*dopt* two kids!

Twice the same driver almost hit me—assuming I'd pause so he could turn. A young couple hoisted girls on their shoulders and started talking monkey language. A pigeon in City Hall Park looked sick and would bat its eyes when you stepped close. A lady with an enormous bosom stood staring at some prewar building. The gas lanterns were on. I admired how a butch woman set off seemingly incompatible shades of blue. Picketers blended in beside one bookstore chain. A cigarette burned from the windowsill.

TUESDAY

By 8:26 it felt almost steamy. Someone had smashed the lobby door again. A spiderman dangled, missing an arm. A box had been addressed to Gretchen A. Fagg. A boy waiting for the bus wore bright blue sneakers which seemed to make him extra shy. A crooked stencil on Fifth Ave. read: They stole us/ They sold us/ Reparations!/ Now!

The Taft Homes looked cleanest higher up. Most people kept their curtains drawn. But the longer I looked I saw narrow slits, with hands moving near kitchen sinks. A fireman swung his arm to stop me as Firetruck 119 lumbered past. It wasn't in any rush but the sirens wailed anyway. I watched how when pigeons and sparrows dart across firehouse lawn they only acknowledge their own species.

As I turned, two commuter trains purred out of sight. A tall kid said I've been doing com*mer*cials. His friend just squinted, defensive maybe. I thought it might be fun to push north under train tracks. It was (but not in a way you remember). Graffiti on a power box read Ghetto Inmates.

A vacant lot on Lexington lay full of two-liter Schweppes bottles. Suburban-looking duplexes had front plots covered in security signs. A bank encouraged renters to put down 3% and buy condos. A battery melted into the sidewalk like an egg. A person all in white presumed I'd checked him out sexually. He frowned. The gravel lot behind him had just been combed.

In the CVS plaza one man cried Violence *is* something; Violence is *some*thing. A sexy Thai girl's photograph printed on a McDonald's cup rolled against a sewer grate. My right contact was presenting persistent problems.

I couldn't figure out the Triborough Bridge. During this delay I felt exposed, foolish, daunted. Traffic bore down on me like a waterfall. A sign halfway up the ramp commanded Keep Walking/ No Lingering Between Signs. I looked out to where grackles flickered on beams. Across Bronx Kill a lot of burning waste shimmered.

Randall's Island split into baseball fields. Shrink-wrapped police boats lined its harbor. I wanted to at least touch ground but construction noise made me turn back early.

Third Avenue felt the most family friendly. There were stable-looking clothes shops, girls in pink jackets. One boy leaned from a stroller so delighted about pigeons he appeared to get stuck. One gay man felt up a giggly acquaintance. She stepped through shattered lobby doors which smelled like tequila.

A mural depicted Puerto Rican boats under the caption New York Love's Rite-Aid. A Corona salesman stood flipping a quarter. Mini-schoolbus drivers jotted descriptions of contorted individuals waiting in wheel-chairs. One sticker with a dog in trenchcoat read Safe Spot: Lugar Seguro. More Lugar Seguro stickers started popping up. A round-faced girl pulled red, green and blue tamales from a vat (each smelled different).

On my return through Taft Homes a calm guy my age whom I've seen many times sipped coffee. A trim woman told another We *should* quit. We're not getting younger. But when you're high it takes the pain away.

My eyes stopped on a puzzle piece. The sixtyish Brazilian hurried past singing. Two unrelated newspaper scraps had melded into a rough-hewn heart. Turning right I stepped near a pair of headphones flattened to the pavement, turning bronze. A tall sexy cop and I looked away as we approached the 4-5-6. A sweet girl in cornrows smiled at the street. I can't decide if the back of my building borders Lincoln State Corrections. It's hard to follow alleys up here because of all the fences.

WEDNESDAY

I shoved my way onto Greenwich at 8:39. It felt as though scissors had lodged in my hip. Pivoting forward like a compass I waved cars through the intersection. People without umbrellas stood straight or dropped their glance to the curb. I think it was a class difference. My hat caught in a stray umbrella tine. When I tried to free it a glove got snagged. Under an awning I yanked at these benign objects—my friends almost.

On the walk to the river I passed a retirement-home café where residents could buy their own big orange juice cartons. When a woman checked me out her partner's eyes defocused. The type of hail falling didn't bounce off streets like marbles. Still I dropped my plan to head north along the Hudson, not wanting to hobble amid hail and traffic and pain.

In Nelson Rockefeller Park the gardener frowned (but only because he loved his plants so much). The bathrooms seemed padlocked with a sign pointing south. A saffron air pocket drifted past. I leaned towards the sudsy water for explanation. A Hoboken ferry looked stripped like meat carcasses in Dutch still-lifes. As the boat docked, this blur cohered into photos of a Bangladeshi woman in chains. I fell in with a pack of ferry commuters. Each held a silent snowflake aura. At Vessey everyone turned east.

In the World Financial Center Mall, under palm trees, people avoiding rain spread newspapers on benches, sat beside paper coffee cups. One tabloid posted a frowning black man on its cover beneath the title What A Dunce! A disaster-recovery display showed mute footage of Governor Pataki at a press conference. Two workers in tan jumpsuits jogged across the lobby. The woman clamped a cigarette between her lips.

Beyond revolving doors stood sand-filled flowerpot ashtrays. These reminded me of arroyos. My right foot hit a puddle (dampening both pant cuffs). Rocks held down garbage can lids. Coins people had tossed onto pylons turned green. Whitecaps didn't disappear the moment you spotted them. Cobblestone mortar lines swirled with rainwater.

I strode parallel to a slightly chubby bald man in rough-cut leather jacket, curious if he was representative of our times. Urban instinct led to a covered footbridge across the West Side Highway. A Thai mom cruised ahead with her sandals clapping her foot soles. A musing Japanese woman lurched. Each female had attained her best possible complexion. Some bulged their eyes as if fighting off sleep. Cars below had headlights on. It wasn't something I would notice from the sidewalk. To the north I scanned the Trade Center pit—a tiny shed and orange cones looked quaint.

Along the Church St. platform someone speaking Korean shifted before a camera and suddenly appeared huge. In the World Trade Center PATH station a woman couldn't believe I didn't want a free paper. A rapping METRO clerk paused to gesture behind a rolling cart. A French man broke from his family, crept between columns, brought his son insane delight.

I dropped onto the longest escalator. The steel high above was haunting. The ride back to mezzanine wasn't as exciting. My heart shuddered, sensing bad 9-11 air.

Arrows pointed down a passage marked Chambers Street. To me that means Kristin. Commuters hurried, clearly distressed, while other people plodded along telling jokes. A humming fenced-off E train sighed. A woman with breasts boggling leered as she passed. This dank neon stretch continued for blocks.

On the return to street level my zipper wouldn't budge. From a lobby a man barked orders in his phone. But it turned out not to be raining now: hoisted umbrellas were just a residue.

THURSDAY

I couldn't leave until 10:06. A crane pivoted with clamped drywall overhead. A surprising amount of wet tobacco fanned out from one crushed Parliament.

Assuming this the last snow of spring I crossed right into Central Park. Already the whitest patches lay pocked. Thawing branches made it feel like rain. Green shoots cleared the soggy drifts. Geese picked through the slush for grass. A seagull corkscrewed down to the water. I questioned a flock of freckled gulls: Do you migrate? Are you terns? About twenty flew off, circled back with one dissonant individual complicating the symmetry.

In the Gardens goopy ice still covered bushes. A stoned groundskeeper said 10-4. His partner's walkie-talkie amplified the phrase. My hip pain sharpened. My gait tightened. The plaque on a bench read Copywriter's Rest. Storm battered crocuses made successful flowers. Blushed violets continued to wilt. A sliced-in-half worm uncoiled. A silver balloon in a barren plot reminded me I'd dreamt of silver. On the way out I wanted to assist one Spanish couple consulting maps.

The Academy of Medicine's iron grate cast calligraphic shadows. The Times covered the latest Pro Life fiasco instead of legitimate news. Hadn't ten oil-refinery workers died in a plant explosion? Where are Christian vigils to support plant safety regulations?

Boys stepped from Mt. Sinai bearing visitors' badges. A man on his way in reeked of cologne. Square wooden crosses near St. Nicholas Orthodox made me internally quiet and serious. I watched a woman lift the gate outside a salon, something I'd never seen a woman do. A separate woman asked her sister Why do you have to make me so *con*scious about it?

As I approached a bakery a gleaming pick-up clicked like its alarm was about to sound. The muffins didn't look excessively sugared. The dj banter clarified my mood. The line spaced me out though. I had to keep walking.

From Madison somebody examining my face smiled just enough so I could respond if I wanted. A gush of ice-melt poured off a blue awning. A crossing guard bulged her eyeballs and joked (kids laughed without really having heard).

My walk flowed to the 96th Street Library. One slight man complained about Thursday's crummy hours. His bag hung held together by safety pins. An SUV with a turn-signal flashing continued straight through the light, so close my face felt it. A particularly composed woman made me flinch/duck inside a clothing store entrance—what was I reacting to? A mom called Hey you're crazy for climbing up there. Her son stood on a giant flowerpot. His sister smiled looking up. There were newly installed daffodils.

The backs of all the Friedrich air conditioners made me think of Nietzsche. Inside a boutique a cashier checked his profile. A clerk tied her own French braids. Both kept talking simultaneously.

The dirt trail I tried to take home ended on smoldering mulch. The distant high-rises rippled. I shouldered a rutted maintenance path, feeling like an arsonist. I reached for a navy-colored balloon halfway down a staircase and slipped. When I turned over the wrinkled balloon it read Feliz Cumpleaños. A lady yanked a mutt's leash yelling Enough already with the chickenbones! A blond informed his frenchie it was time to settle down.

FRIDAY

I held the door for an Arabic man but he lingered far behind. I turned west and a walk came to me. At 9:12 the air felt loose and gray. A hairdresser had hung her posters askew. An exhausted blonde handing over spare change spun off when the guy started to tell his story. From a small, low sports car sprang the percussive buildup to "1999." Part of me surged.

A neglected John Hancock statue looked very plain anyway. A suspicious black man in a fez cap glared. I passed many churches, forgetting names, unable to read whole titles. It was scary when a jogger caught up from behind. One quaint sign just read Chop Suey.

A tall German girl wearing a lot of skin cream smiled as we passed on the climb up Convent. Somebody asked someone stapling preschool flyers several meandering questions. He was obviously trying to pick her up. From church steps a man called Seventy-five *years*! You bet I'm happy! A dressed up boy on the opposite stoop ate an apple adorably.

Random snow lingered on just one block. I smiled when a maimed Chinese student passed. Afterwards I regretted this. I took my hat off and the hair stood up like a shell.

Joy as I continued up Convent couldn't find any cause at first. Then the flushed brownstones started. Stained-glass details made the morning delicate. A carpenter carried his level straight. I felt an insane desire to confirm I'd seen gas lamps. I crossed to inspect the one lit porch (as if I couldn't tell this was electric light). A tour group outside the Alexander Hamilton Museum took interest. A stout Native American wrapped his arm around a banker, led the guy into a Lincoln Continental.

I pictured parks coming around 146th. A church front resembled a huge concrete slide. There wasn't any park. I soon turned east. A stripped mansion stood at the corner facing another entitled Dawn Hotel. Burning plastic fumes left me faint. A man selling Black Power fists stopped as I crossed. A magic-markered sign read Head Start Closed (Good Friday).

Along St. Nick's Park I passed crocus shoots sprinkled with torn cups, lotto tickets, pens. Workers swept debris down Convent Hill. An androgynous art student climbing the staircase looked especially slender beside her portfolio. Someone had colored certain squares on stone chess-tables pink and blue.

In front of the Lionel Hampton Towers a dog wore a homemade cheetah-print top. I said Hi to the owner. She didn't look. Four guys split apart to let me pass. One kept bouncing his basketball so hard it sailed above him. A funeral home kept stretching along the bottom of one apartment house. This took up at least four awnings.

From 125th I was still unsure whether to make cars stop when I had the right of way, since only white people seemed to hold such expectations. Scaffold graffiti just said Rip Dice. A man with an earring had to drag one foot. A guava juice sat on a payphone ledge. Across Frederick Douglass a girl poked her friend and pointed up at a Fanta sign. It showed one woman dressed in orange sway beside another in purple.

The flyer in a Senegalese café presented a crouched boy karate-kicking barefoot above his afro. When the man in front paused I also hesitated—shifting keys from coat pocket to pants. One spaced-out girl stared off pressing a lobby intercom. One shy woman passed shielding wildly bucked teeth. One neighbor wound a wheelchair through the plaza, gave his gregarious dog some exercise.

I thought about the land and wanted to care for it.

MONDAY

I spun out behind two smoke-black shaggy dogs. Before getting an umbrella up at 8:46 cool drops had seeped through my collar. On her erratic dash down Warren a woman used awnings as shields. I watched kids get greeted in Park Dayschool. I turned and almost stepped in a stroller pushed by an attractive blond mother wearing plaid. The shyness of the encounter sexualized it. Stores stood quiet because of rain.

By Chambers I felt caught in someone's weekend summary: So these dudes fell a*sleep*...we went on the roof to talk...finally they came up and were just total *ass*holes. Stains spread down buildings like a Clyfford Still. Four women bunched beside the Cosmopolitan Hotel communicated a non-verbal friendliness my way. I think it was weird for us to be around thirty. A scruffy guy clutched his blanket and watched it pour. Behind, somebody had pasted sepia scraps into a person.

On Walker a kid with his arm in a sling smoked a rain-pocked cigarette. A terrier took a running leap off the curb. An obviously intelligent African boy carried his drooped umbrella like a broken wing. A ruddy white person's snapped, but he flipped it straight and used what was left. Fence behind him opened on an earthy pit. Men amid construction vehicles murmured in groups of two and four.

One basset hound wouldn't step beyond an awning. The owner used his foot as a spatula. The dog's red eyes lacked pupils. The adjacent boutique announced Endless Possibilities. A grid of sixteen pictures portrayed a black woman and a white woman bonding, admiring a rocky seascape, alternating neutral tones.

A girl in yellow boots pushed her sister's stroller. Though I didn't recognize the mom I assumed she once modeled. A Chinese girl practiced landing in puddles. Rapids running down the curb reminded me of a guitar's bridge. The dots comprising a pedestrian figure now reminded me of raindrops. The Community Gardens north of Houston hadn't greened. Moisture beaded along a bush and its berries. Plangent garlic aroma hovered. Fiorello De La Guardia's pediment flickered with constant rain taps.

By Washington Square my cords clung at the shins. A teen nosed his way under a friend's umbrella, made me miss getting through the whole day flirting. After someone kissed his pink-haired girlfriend goodbye her smile lingered. The rain running down deli windows reminded me of carwashes. The scaffolds sufficed where women lay beneath a puffy blue bedspread.

On the walk back my intuitions sharpened. When I forked left a sparrow splattered puddles with its wings. NYU's solid Near Eastern Studies Center compelled me to want to work on that subject. For the first time I passed NYU Law, appraised the life I almost chose as students frowned at mist. Bacony scents wafted out The Peanut Shop's cellar. Townhouses on Sullivan alternated where the doorways were. I peeked up one landing to where pigeons sounded glad. My toes hit water (cool flush felt right).

Near Houston a valet hurried around a double-parked silver limousine, handing off his umbrella just in time. It turned out to be a hearse trailed by low-beamed cars. The boss said We can't open the goddamn door like this Freddy; you're gonna have to back them all up. Freddy splashed down the block shouting Everyone's got to back up ten feet. But by the time he reached the procession's end there was a delivery truck with hazards on.

I passed a Greenstreets plot lined with bicycle taxis. I hallucinated blond flames coming from a flower. Approaching signs that said Organic I thought I smelled waffles—but the windows opened on an abstract salon. An Islamic couple pushed a baby carriage. Their voices evoked being happy in a city. The woman's headdress traced marble doves. A loud red restaurant I normally disdain had filled one entrance with Easter violets. A ladder led down a manhole reeking of cigars. A twelve-year-old sat at a Park Dayschool desk, surrounded by much smaller kids.

TUESDAY

At 8:50 I could finger dew off cars. The Dana Discovery custodian called out Hi. Swans slept on the driest rocks. Mallards tailed a band of albino ducks. A goose chomping grass stopped and stared at me sideways. *Pardon* I said but it hissed then clambered off like a man in flippers.

The park had returned to overall green. I thought about the land and wanted to care for it. Macho joggers had on shorts. An old guy carried a satchel of rushes. Beeps announced a van was backing up. Heads bobbed along the reservoir fence. A cop asked somebody cute in running tights What's your mutt's name? and she said Alex.

Strangers talked at bus stops, scanning the street. Lines sprawled down The Met's stairs but I guessed it wasn't crowded. From a bench somebody delirious filled out applications. Someone Middle Eastern sneezed while fastening together a t-shirt display. Someone else Middle

Eastern smiled setting up soda cans, got serious when a woman crossed in red rubber boots.

Suffering mild daytime vertigo I bent and scratched a dog's wet snout. When the owner laughed her lipstick felt close to my eyeballs. A squat man hobbled from the Indonesian Embassy as if one leg was a cane. Are you waiting for a cab? he asked a woman at the corner. *Non Non* she beamed, pawing him, clearing space on the curb. A private-school boy passed puffing his lips, practicing for the bassoon maybe.

On the Hunter College steps I trailed two beige-skinned men bearing irises. From the Lexington Ave. skywalk I saw a girl bind her wrists with a rainbow scarf. Low-beam headlights couldn't cut through the gloom. I dropped off *Rings of Saturn* and *Lucy Church Amiably*. I didn't acknowledge the library guard. But opposite a tall woman all in gold I fought a strange compulsion to say Thank you. Instead I murmured Morning: no response. I signed out on a photocopy pickup too lazy to really write my last name.

In Shakespeare's Books, as a clerk found my shelf, I listened to "A Hard Rain's Gonna Fall" on bootleg, was moved and wondered about the sixties, felt a part of something external and alive. Almost weeping I filled out the form for my complimentary copy of Claudia Rankine.

Across 68th a woman's stride suggested muscular discomfort with skirts. When the light changed I tried to match her pace. I cut through liquor boxes stacked overhead.

From the ATM alcove of an old-fashioned bank I overheard customers requesting things, then the tellers sat busy and the hall felt buoyant. A shy man twisted some special device and parking-meter change dropped into his cup. A staring pregnant woman seemed to wonder if I was kind. A Korean girl's waist gleamed when she bent to gather laundry bags. She glanced as I reached the windowsill.

At the 96th St. Public Library I dropped off *One Train* and *John Cage Reads John Cage*. I fled with my body scrunched in case the clerk called me back for late fees. Still I grabbed state tax forms. A teenage couple made out from the steps and it was for some reason sexier because they both had zits.

Continuing west I passed a blotchy man whose lips wagged constantly like a fish's. A giggling Mexican caterer had an insulated hotbox strapped to his chest. In Gourmet Garage I sampled Moroccan Olives, Spanish Olives with Cumin, Brown Rice Crispy Squares. Careful this one's got a little chipotle the clerk said as he passed a spoon of chicken salad. Amid narrow aisles that made my muscles clench I heard "Orange Crush," then a catchy Van Morrison tune, then something recent and kind of quiet by The Boss. It was obviously weird I didn't have a cart so I gave up shoplifting bagels. The cashier's skin glowed within the calm of the store. I regretted gross fingernails scraping against her palm.

When a Hasid almost hit me I screamed through his window. This passed so fluidly I never was upset. Cafeteria cooks smoked behind a brown dumpster. Each stood dressed entirely in maroon. A redhead's tights made me feel pliant. A businesswoman my age smiled as we passed. A boy with a plaid suitcase stared at the park (his upside-down umbrella reminded me of musicals).

WEDNESDAY

Beyond the courtyard people passed and I felt the day through their posture. It was 9:26 and warm when the air stirred. For the first time this spring I wore an oxford with the sleeves rolled. Honking geese set off pleasant vibrations inside me like a Stravinsky concerto for woodwinds. Floating ducks sat distributed in a way that made The Meer look extra big. Someone Chinese laid a cane along a bench, followed her fingers for eye exercise. Somebody walked ahead of a maintenance van unhooking emergency ice-break ladders. Someone else pulled the spikes on which ladders had hung. A jogger gyrated through a sexy form of push-ups. I held my breath then sort of gasped spotting brown skin against concrete. In a reedy corner police barricades stood ready to be deployed.

A groundskeeper pondered which branch to trim then tore through like a savage. A blonde removed scraps with a pair of pincers. A frizzy woman wore purple: lipstick, earrings. Screechy bus brakes swarmed my attention. Another bus stopped to let a woman step off with her cane, a mother carry a daughter off on her shoulders, a stylish old woman glide down erect.

A sunny gap between high-rises smelled like cleanser and made me sneeze. Under a random black plume of smoke kids lined up in gray sweatshirts. One short girl kept jumping to whisper to a friend. One Haitian woman stared off pushing a white boy's swing—just for a second though, then she was sweet to him. From a bench two guys in business suits screamed Hola! at everyone.

A fiftyish woman walked a bike past The Met with a pant leg tucked in her sock. A tour guide sitting on bus steps wore a Times Square tie with an apple at its center. A phalanx of girls smiled down from the staircase. Chaperones took pictures with dozens of cameras.

In the sixties I passed a police-chase film set too dumb to describe. I blanked until through mesh canopies I sensed exotic birds. A black goat bent around a wall to stare at me. Its mother looked porcelain and edible. As a zookeeper approached with pellets in her palm goats lined the fence nudging faces. Behind them a pig shook straw off its back, all except one strand. I turned to catch a mom watching me; we smiled.

At the park's south edge stood more barricades. I peeked inside The Plaza (which didn't feel famous). Someone not naturally attractive had altered herself in a charcoal suit. Someone working-class peered into a van's hood. His dusty sweatshirt was like the sky before dawn. A boy strapped to a father rubbed balloons against his leg. Another boy clung to this same dad's arm. A teenage girl stomped, convinced her family was headed in the wrong direction. A heavy woman from the South said Look hon there's an H&M.

The giant inflatable union rat pointed its claws at Trump Tower. Local One Elevator had been locked out. Workers swelled behind barricades. Daughters distributed flyers. Tourists stepped closer to crop all this from pictures. A homeless man made birdcalls. For half a block it smelled like eucalyptus. For the same length a quote from the Mahabharata stretched along a clothing store.

In front of a bank, beside a damp woman sprawled asleep on one elbow, Japanese girls squatted studying maps. Men spun around with boards on their chests advertising buffets and computer parts. One passed me a flyer with a snapping sound. The melody from "It's a Hard Knock Life" coursed through my head though I never saw the movie *Annie*. The lilies in Rockefeller Center reminded me of gramophones. Stooping tourists with cameras reminded me of old-fashioned cameras with curtains and tripods.

Across 35th a couple folded against seatbelts, wanting to see some building tops. A pair of discarded jeans made a tidy bundle along the curb. The do-ragged driver of a Heineken truck stopped to talk with a woman smoking. Behind him car horns went crazy. Noise peaked just when I turned into school under rippling ads for The Gap.

THURSDAY

Soft air at 7:46 made me want always to stay calm. Workers next door played salsa. Both dumpsters overflowed. Where I crossed 110th Catholic schoolboys sprinted. The kid in front glanced sideways to make sure he kept his lead. A large green apple rolled to the curb. Snow piles made The Meer feel sort of like an ashtray. Cabs curving while climbing through the park evoked Edward Hopper and horses. I didn't walk Central Park West as planned. I hate traffic speeding in the opposite direction. I dropped along a dirt path below the mossy park wall.

Twigs glistened against the slope as if iced. The glinting came from broken glass (more than I'd ever seen). There were also eviscerated cigarette lighters. Two birders passed, withholding focus. I knew I lacked talent for finding birds. Two gardeners gossiped from parallel carts. A stuffed pink dinosaur sat beside one. Sparrows rooted amid woodchips, made scavenging together sound sweet and attractive.

Ascending Great Hill I met two black poodles—one with whitening paws. I passed Abraham Lincoln on a newspaper scrap. Lawns shimmered like a friend's bangs when the sun hits from certain angles. Two dogs chasing each other snarled as they came close. A woman who'd had a face-lift cradled a puppy biting its collar. She stood orbited by four tempestuous bichons. Far ahead on the track a jogger called out Sandy! Sandy sprinted around the curve. When her owner spun around and jogged backwards Sandy even accelerated.

Workers swept a tennis court with tools with round black heads. Debris lay just beyond the baselines. A couple in mismatch sweats volleyed soundly. There were really tiny bags I associate with drugs.

The grooved East Meadow softball diamonds suggested infinite concentricity. Robins picked through fenced-off outfields. As I cut on a downhill diagonal towards the Loch the skewed perspective felt refreshing. An Indian boy pouted with boredom as his preppy elders examined The Ravine. North Woods seemed thin with winter gone (like a wet dog's skinny legs). My eyes stopped where a woodpecker gorged itself. Larvae tumbled down its tongue. Over the last several days someone had carved Bobby in a stair along the waterfall.

Coming out onto Lasker Rink the ice looked drier than expected, much more like what's in a freezer. Nearby a hose leaked steadily. A shy, pony-tailed park worker made a point of saying Hello.

Back at The Meer a turtle surfaced. Its legs dangled in shafts of sunny water. When I stopped to look it dove out of light but a new kind of alternative duck swept past: blue-billed, slant-eyed, with punk rock hair.

A rabbit appeared in a hand-stitched bonnet. Its owner stared as if waiting for me to smile. Something vanished, leaving foam. Someone rollerblading with gay strokes said Isn't it a gift man? I saw that it was. A woman who had seemed reserved sprinted around the pond followed by a shih tzu. From one bench somebody explained in his phone There's a lot of shit I'm walkin' with…and it's hard.

A silhouetted bird spun enormous wings as if to ease tension in its shoulder blades. I prepared for an eagle. It was just a normal goose. Three kids ran toward me with the girl constantly adjusting her face so that tiny red sunglasses didn't fall off.

From a pick-up someone Jamaican called Aha! Good to see you again! Now forget the jacket because it's not cold anymore! Passing a neighbor I pursed my lips, not wanting to confuse him saying hi from the street.

FRIDAY

Kristin and I spun out onto chalky construction at 8:16. One ankle still felt raw against the sock after yesterday's somersault off my bike. But with my nostrils steaming as we parted I felt immortal. Behind Il Giglio a compact truck held thousands of starched white blouses. A toddler watched his preschool's gate rise. It seemed unhealthy for a child to be so patient. Passing parking lots I calculated how much money they brought in: based on rates and number of slots. But what did I care? What did I feel following a billboard-sized horizontal woman reflected off a Spanish restaurant? Would Freud have called it flattery?

Atop the roof of an idling van stood Snack Packs with the coldcuts uneaten. The driver slept with his mouth wide open. At the next van someone sipped coffee, stared ahead as if steering.

Outside City Hall somebody swerved, straining to get around an old couple. The State Courthouse on Centre had had its steps removed. Flyers directing citizens to a Pearl Street side-entrance faded into rainbows after last night's storm. Men clutching cardboard filecases looked healthy but close to anachronistic. A black boy asked how to get in the building. A bewildered mom was picked to be searched.

On Canal I stood waiting for the light to change beside a Mexican girl whose boot heels glimmered. Ahead a white person twitched at the elbows. His arms hung stretched out stiff like clotheslines. Examining a crossing-guard's wrinkled slacks I wondered how many uniforms they gave her. The embossed fabric looked thicker than anything I own.

Continuing north I saw a Singer sewing machine sur-rounded by sepia scissor-packages from China. I assumed discs priced $10 a pound were stingrays. A bunch of fork-lifts scooped crates of skinned pigs. The garage they backed into reeked of incense. Throbbing blue hoses discharged eels with the eels slithering even as they fell.

A Latin Dance studio's gaudy sign got me thinking about the neighborhood three flights up. A tan woman walked parallel to me, both of us smiling while staring straight. The way her heels clicked seemed so self-impor-tant. I slowed to consider rusty bikes locked together along a takeout joint. I stood surrounded by produce boxes with a composite smell of strawberry. Half a block before Houston somebody held small flags from his window. A quarter-block later someone napped with face wedged under a grocery cart. A chained flowerpot crumbled at its base. A waitress had triceps not toned in a gym.

Across Great Jones two brittle black men filled out applications from a spa's steps. The standpipes had spikes so you couldn't sit. One guy looked sloppy tearing posters from scaffolds (I'd assumed long strips would peel right off). On Elizabeth Street, inside a sports car crammed with orange juice boxes, one person slept, hugging himself. Elizabeth's lawn of porcelain statues disarmed me, because at first it resembled a cemetery, then it became the most open, least used, quietest yard for miles. An inscription about the police department had disintegrated more than any plaque I'd ever seen—as if crowds tossed acid on it for decades.

Two Chinese clerks waved through a window, startled white kids staring at them. I slowed to a distracting pace behind someone translucent with a half-pint of milk. His fingers couldn't close around shopping bag handles. Cold men smoked and huddled selling fresh fish. A sheet contained handwritten characters beneath somebody's passport photo. A cellar-door conveyor belt bleated like a lamb.

Outside Red Dragon Extermination Agency an old man's bike tipped but he just went on talking; the fall had been cushioned by a lettuce box. From Columbus Park's southern edge a woman fed scraps to a tin drum fire. Fumes left me dizzy. I sat surrounded by rice bowls, half with egg. Someone staring at a storefront checked his zipper. Though it hadn't started raining girls shared an umbrella. A van bumped then ended up dragging a cone.

Torn $12 stackable chairs suggested I was back in Tribeca. Tall Tribeca Works men passed with brown suits the texture of sleeping bags. Filling the line along Javits Courthouse were just the people you'd expect: modest, stunned. The only grinning person chewed on a plastic fork.

A turtle craned its neck…

MONDAY

Six people rode the elevator down (a record). I exited Kristin's at 8:29. Boys paced before a school as though they'd never met. My blood felt cold far beneath the skin. Pedestrians grimaced or faced away from each other. The only bikers wore facemasks.

Near the Hudson a mini-golf course smelled like tires. Aspens tipped on a couple greens. Somebody silhouetted watched barges. Someone bald looked embarrassed to photograph the river's surface. The trapeze academy for adults was four bare towers and a shed. The bike-rental stand sat shuttered. Passing lines of flexible posts I fought off the urge to slalom.

Pylons rose from water conflating perspectives, like Klimt's paintings of trees. A floating branch reminded me of antlers. Another stuck straight up like a spear. The western sky seemed a separate river. I passed a bundle of mini Stop signs and fences stacked into one thick curve. Pier 40 gently buzzed. Beyond its gate a sports field glowed. From his shed a security guard smiled like he'd have let me in if he could.

Big wooden doors bulged painted a blue I always love walking along. A party boat I'll often see crowded bobbed on slurpy cables. I peeked through a rusty slit into a warehouse. The emptiness hung iridescent with river echoes and light. The highest windows had duct-tape x's.

From the pier's westernmost point I felt about a third of the way to New Jersey. The Lackawanna sign hummed so that I could have sat staring. Benches constructed of recyclable plastic were almost the same as wood. A startled jogger asked How are you? but didn't slow down.

Stenciled fish led to kiosks for announcements and awards. Photos showed city kids freezing in canoes. A kayaker brooded but maintained a swift pace. A floating volleyball spun amid trash. With a little water in front of it Tribeca looked just like Hoboken. A dog I never saw sneezed.

On Houston a pigeon stalked near traffic, only once pecking at a bag. Graffiti showed someone point a finger-gun at his temple. Surrounding captions read New York Needs A Release, Religion Is Laziness, Shivering In The Night. Palpable darkness as I crossed through garages resembled a pause between film reels. Peeled-off poster scraps sank into sidewalk. Twins jogged in place as trucks pulled out.

Just below Canal someone paused to smoke the instant his suitcase cleared a vestibule. His shirt flapped dramatically unbuttoned. He was forty. A Taiwanese woman with a hardhat crouched above a computer. A stylish mom screamed Good*bye*! into a phone without actual momentum. A spotted dog turned to bark at another once their masters separated.

On Duane I passed a patisserie in which I've always envied everyone. I cut into Washington Market Park— where the playground apparatus expands each spring. I circled the fenced-off grass wondering if fuzz meant cherries were about to bloom. The gazebo could be reserved again. The sight of a shed made me want to talk with somebody. It bothered me most spruce had browned.

In the New York Sports Club a woman on a tread-mill hunched highlighting a passage. Steps before Kristin's I closed my eyes. Whirrings and drills surrounded me. There was an architectural order to these sounds. It felt like a train slowed, creaking overhead. Two figures in face-masks varnished the lobby.

TUESDAY

I left convinced I wouldn't want a jacket. But at 8:36 it wasn't true. Triple-ply windows leaned against Lincoln Corrections Facility. I looked back and felt boxed out of life. As an old woman disappeared behind maintenance trucks I heard her call out Morning. Continuing counter-clockwise around The Meer she discovered a playground's Euclidean calm. A pigeon landed near somebody's bicycle tire. Hownk hownk! the middle-aged rider screamed. Get out of my way dumb bird.

Sun rippling off water made nearby stones pulse. In one flowerbed swaths of daffodils had bloomed. In others individual shoots had sprung. Either scene made me want to shout Yes! One goose looked stunned and puritanical standing on a rock with wet black feet. One male duck crept towards a napping female who paddled off. One flashing police car pushed me up into a fence. I was shivering.

The Conservatory Gardens' bathroom seemed poignant and appealing, smelling of spring and zoos. Amid chattering park workers I felt aimless. Clusters of tulips and narcissi (Marilyn, Jetfire) took shape as they climbed. Shredded plastic caught in branches made me think Francis Scott Key.

Kids signed exams against a school wall. A maroon van's dashboard read C-L-E-R-G-Y in gothic font. A homeless guy flipped to the Times Op-Ed. An attractive woman stepped from the laundromat saying So *then* I told him I think you have *prob*lems and need to seek *help*. A mounted jaguar photograph was somehow the portrait of a sexy vain boy. A man crossed Third Ave. with his dog's sparkly heart-shaped tags tinkling. A sparrow fumbled then flew off with either a cheeto or cigarette filter.

Along the East River Projects somebody in a wheelchair said I *can't* I um got a building inspection. It sounded like he was stalling. Grackles fought over fried-eggplant strips which probably none would end up eating. Out of pure altruism I told one shy girl I really like your dachshund.

As always when I hit the East River an adult with a German shepherd jogged but paths otherwise lay empty. In front of Ward's Island the water's shimmer pulled apart. A faded sign read S dium. A band of tiny alternative ducks both slept and looked out for each other. Turning north I felt sunbeams sparkle in my hair. Paint peeled off the 111th St. Bridge in giant strips like wallpaper. Tulip bulbs from the shadows swayed.

Windshield wipers held parking tickets along tiered, middle-income housing projects I always forget the name of. One car with the proper permit had its windshield shattered. Someone had drawn an ironic dick on the hood. Somebody's van passed airbrushed with the names of famous musicians: Celia Cruz, Tito Puente. Other themes for this vehicle were Puerto Rico and Fireman.

Atop a security camera above 112th a sparrow scratched behind the ear. A mom walked between two boys so small she could barely reach them. From the corner someone called Hey gorgeous sunshine how you feeling? Beyond him a mural placed martinis beside crashed sportscars oozing blood. Clean-shaven models in foodstamp ads made me think I might qualify. Two sparrows shared a pizza slice without any cheese or tomato sauce left. Two men cried No fucking way! and Holy shit! as they approached. Others gathered around a Peruvian woman pouring tan liquid (not coffee) into paper cups.

After dozens of commutes to a distant library I found the local branch 4 blocks east. I got dirty looks brushing against double-parked cars. A sign near the bus stop announced $2000 Penalties For Idling Engines. Its symbol suggested global warming. Finally, I thought.

Men dropped garbage bags from a second-story patio (gently: so they wouldn't split). On my way past Lincoln Corrections a guard burst out giggling, said Reminds me of something happened at home last night. He coughed and couldn't elaborate.

WEDNESDAY

Because I first had to brush my teeth I left Kristin's hungry and forgot to check the time. This was around 9:50. Gee Whiz Diner customers salted eggs with neutral faces. A liquor store's mopped tiles dried against the breeze. Most people stood balanced by headphones and a paper coffee cup. Some had bare arms.

Crossing Hudson I hallucinated oncoming cabs. I just was panicking because the intersection's not perpendicular. A woman under an awning explained I had a second, so I thought I'd call. A couple with a baby frowned, cold, seated at the Belgian pub's sidewalk table and I wondered if this is always the case. A boy propped in a sixth-floor bedroom talked by phone with women at the curb. I wondered why he didn't poke his head out and scream. A deliveryman bent comparing a customer's printout against his own pink copy, blinked to signify confusion.

Two teenage moms asked directions to Franklin so faintly I almost kept walking. Stylish young people in a plot below Canal were actually engineers discussing where to set a fountain. Squat men whose ethnicity I couldn't place leaned parallel to the street, pushing a creaky Sabrett cart through a red light as a bus approached. Further up Thompson French sous chefs lingered, exhaled (gathering momentum to unlock the front door). Somebody African steered a forklift from a trailer. He seemed to smile and begin showing off. Behind him voices yelled Cut! Cut!

The dog that I asked How long have you been tied? turned to follow my progress past a deli. A dark cat framed by iron grids preempted any question with a yellow stare. As I burst past an Australian he said in his phone Take all the time you want honey. This made me feel bad—I'd stuck an arm up between us to imply a wall.

Just south of Washington Square smelled tropical. Orange snowplows stood stacked facedown. Ahead someone on a cane shouted It's *Stan*ley. I'm at NYU.

Pushing north I passed two chess players with 25 and 19 seconds remaining. A girl stopped to ask the time. As I felt though my backpack for my phone she wanted to bond about us not wearing watches. I wondered if what we were approaching was the Flatiron Building.

Turning left I trailed kids in Red Sox shirts. Two had open facial cuts. I slowed to get away from their aggressive voices. Other pedestrians did the same. Finally I let everyone leave me behind, watched a sparrow call out from the traffic light. A thick chain strung around hyacinths only attached to itself.

Across Sixth Ave. tall blond women with briefcases and high heels sprinted. It felt like a commercial. Once I'd cleared the debris from a Day and Night Rubbish Removal truck I stopped to take off my sweater. One frail black woman set up a sidewalk table. For now there was just vague incense aroma. I glimpsed sky between magnolia blossoms. I slapped the Jefferson Market Library and called it My good friend.

Near 17th I wove through police convoys, partially losing consciousness because of sirens. Beside a bank a fat boy muttered I bet half those assholes don't know where they're driving. Somebody whistled and someone in a short white skirt looked up. She smiled and I crossed Sixth behind her. A rich man squatted reading the Post with a green bandanna and long gray beard. More interested in him now, his phoniness, I barely noticed when construction guys flipped at the short white skirt. One dropped to his knees to better look, but only from far enough away it didn't count.

Mirrors in 26th St. stands depicted Michael Jordan dunking on people. Someone Senegalese pointed fingers and affirmed Yes! This is where you get your bargain! Along Fifth I passed a bus-stop androgyne standing contrapposto like Tadzio (*Death in Venice*). He had braces. Cabs blew hot dust. Someone in a pink mohawk crossed, then I saw the same thing on a phone-booth advertisement, then a nervous woman passed with just pink hair. I'd planned to pause outside the Graduate Center but instead swerved between cigarettes.

THURSDAY

At 8:06 some woman said thanks for letting her in the lobby. She seemed to have been waiting a while. My plan to see both rivers collapsed when I spotted red fuzz in Central Park. A boy split from his girlfriend, spun around and walked backwards. A man stepped stiffly as if he wore clogs. White daffodils made the morning look catered. A sleeping swan looked flat. A mini shipwreck floated in The Meer. I wondered how deep its water got.

Along the opposite shore two denim-clad women turned black against bright sun. Passing a different woman I for no reason tripped and almost staggered into rushes. A plaque about the baldcypress started *These deciduous conifers…* I spaced out on its music. A seagull's wing bled.

Happy Café (concession stand) finally had reopened. As the clerk called Que pasa he worked heavy suds into a plastic counter. A cyclist interrupted this pleasant exchange screaming On your *left*! and my daughter's behind me!

I curved with the Gardens' old brick wall. A female cardinal confirmed why the word smoldering is sexy. Within budding tulips an entire universe seemed to touch. The narcissi resembled girls sticking out their chests.

Workers left the far gate locked; I had to exit on 5th to continue south. Someone passed reading a book which must have been the bible given its font. A separate woman waiting for the bus slapped her palm with a brown umbrella. A two-toned hearse paused, surprisingly short. I took a running leap back into the park.

Where I landed a rich Caribbean lady had a wild silver streak in her hair. Her collie blanked when a pit bull appeared but the pit bull accosted two tinier dogs: overrunning them so it could approach from behind. Two homeless figures lay head to head with hats across the faces. Someone came from bushes carrying a needle. His eyebrows alone would have made me flinch. A boy hoisted a branch like a purpose he'd discovered. This park hollow stayed cooler and mistier than the rest.

Ascending East Meadow ridge I saw Latino men in stride. I guessed they were playing soccer. I dropped down plains wondering how people can flow so well without being more effective on offense—as if secretly no one wanted to score that many goals.

Pigeons cooed inside a sealed stone house along the reservoir. A jogger's Keds made me think Beauty parlor. Another had a rainbow scarf tucked in her spandex. It was all I noticed the next quarter-mile. The water's surface never stopped changing. With distant towers sliding past every moment should have felt complete.

The southern stretch (around 85th) smelled like a small Midwestern lake. This made me feel close to my family. Beyond the joggers on the track's far edge ran two more rings of cross-country people. Two women passed at a similar pace but with totally different bodies. Tan guys' legs glowed against neon shorts. Penguin-looking ducks skidded down, descending on a mallard couple. The female flew away fastest. The others followed her underwater.

One Filipina mom climbing the outer bend spit into shivering leaves yards off. One half-Japanese jogger glimmered through foliage. One dog walker in tight pink t-shirt proved some people don't have to work so hard. Stray irises unfurled as I entered The Ravine. Woodpeckers shared a disintegrating branch. They spun around searching for the right spot to pierce.

Accelerating down steps toward the waterfall I vowed to stride boldly forever. Climbing back to Lasker Rink I met a stocky blue jay. A Thai man watched sparrows from what seemed the perfect distance. A turtle craned its neck from the drying rock.

FRIDAY

From the courtyard I could tell I needed a jacket. On the climb upstairs my throat tingled. I'd hoped storms would temper allergies but Yuki my roommate stood clutching her head.

Finally at 8:56 I passed Puerto Rican girls smoothing bangs before the lobby mirror with Elton John singing "Don't Go Breakin' My Heart" in the background. I turned east under new surveillance cameras. I felt conscious of seagulls' plumpness as they hovered beside lampposts. In front of Schaumburg Towers a hearse driver took his hat off and looked untrustworthy with slick gray hair. Traffic honked behind him. From Duke Ellington Circle I couldn't gauge what was graffiti and what commercial, especially the part that read Chocolate Mami.

Piled garbage bags waited to be gathered. Misery seemed preventable in a city. A pit contained plastic soccer balls with some pentagonal plates missing. A project's grass was the first thing absolutely green. A wrestler doll plummeted then landed face-up. The other white person past Lexington chuckled. She happened to be appealing. Striding along amid her soothing heels it didn't seem right to say we weren't communicating.

I cut down Third past a crowded doughnut shop, curious if windows displayed real bricks or wallpaper. Had landlords given up on this street? A banner promised Tax Return Fa$t. A microwave lay in dew at the curb with the cord neatly wrapped around it. At P.S. 72 (now a Latino Community Center) every ungrated window had been pelted with rocks. Shrieking kid voices echoed up a stairwell. Slavic grandmas stopped and blinked.

I wound through the Gardens. It seemed crazy not to. Familiar bushes abruptly flared yellow. Pollen rippled across walkways like desert sands. Rain-beaten narcissi bent over. I wanted to tell them theirs was a tragic death, like Hamlet's. I hoped crushed stargazers knew they'd died in pairs. Half of what I'd thought were magnolias are really something else. These mystery petals laced the Woodland Slope. A dog walker got vicarious thrill from me: she kept passing just to smile. The only species name I didn't forget was Sweet Harmony (narcissus).

Ascending an unofficial trail I hit soaked stretches and identified with moss. From North Meadow's ridge I looked out—all alone. Single joggers solidified against trees. Groundsworkers leveled the softball diamonds. I pushed west under damp growth and loud birds. As an approaching taxi curved with the drive I decided many events reach me that way.

But surrounded by thick brown marsh I wanted to be home. This never had happened on a previous walk. My girlfriend might move to Massachusetts. Someone's positioned herself to take over my apartment. Next year I'll again have less income than before.

I avoided eye contact with a Canadian couple who obviously wanted their picture taken. They didn't approach the sneezing nun behind me either. Stray yellow clovers restored my secret confidence. Weary boys watched a supervisor distribute gloves.

On church steps opposite the Stranger's Gate someone used a wheelchair as storage locker. A Japanese girl never stopped singing as she passed. It turned out to be much later than expected. Still I took The Meer all the way to Lenox St. Playground. A gate fluttered open. A goose slept on one leg. Another crouched like that staring. The Discovery Center bathrooms looked bleached and civic. The front hall stood silent. I slipped off sneakers not wanting to track mud.

Good luck you guys. It's blustery.

MONDAY

I'd underdressed again but it was too late in spring to bother. Brightness at 8:46 made me sneeze. On the sidewalk I saw the shadow of my agitated hair. A bird's shadow flew over it. Sparrows cut perfect L's as if for love of synchronicity.

Where I crossed the West Side Highway a (boy) jogger's chest jiggled. A crane hoisted flimsy beams. Tribeca had another new red building. New Jersey could have been a barge. I wondered about the Andean wool wraps rich women wear. The boxers I was wearing bunched uncomfortably. I remembered Kristin noticing last night just as we both lost consciousness.

North Cove's cherries still hadn't bloomed. They only looked stunning seen against sky. Then it felt like there was a cello inside me. I thought about how seagulls coast when they can. I contemplated how a security-guard's crooked baton dangled. I pictured the workshop in which she learned to use this weapon. The sun blew streaked with building exhaust.

Grackles picked at Cinnabons laid in a ring. Geometric shadows held their shape against the Hudson. Discharge from a passing tanker suggested some basic engineering principle. Pipes spouted when the river surged. Someone entered the harbor on a rubbery boat—standing up. I watched piers rock until I could sense my organs.

Of four young Europeans bent over a bridge it was hard to tell which one walked with a cane. I slowed and considered fenced-off violets. I resisted stepping in time to an hydraulic drill's pulse. Bloodhounds crouched to avoid conversation. Somebody stretched taut on a bench twitched when his boot strayed over the side. Someone's hi-tech sleeping bag had headphones clamping down the facemask. A tugboat led an enormous freighter. The ship's only Chinese feature was its flag.

West Africans slunk as if they weren't selling watches. The Sabrett salesmen read something like a scroll. The graphic layout of a policeman's magazine confirmed its subject (entertainment). By nine blond families had bought hot pretzels. I wanted to hear harsh Scandinavian sounds but they were from the Midwest. When the river's swell receded it sucked my foot against an iron grate. As this feeling withdrew I missed it. A potato bug crawled out onto concrete. I hadn't seen one in years.

Watching the Staten Island Ferry push off, listening to ropes on nearby ships sigh, I sensed I'm going to move soon—maybe across the water. On my return through Battery Park a man yanked his son's elbow, said Nobody likes a smart aleck. I can't describe the river's color then. It was neither orange nor bronze. Someone else woke wearing normal clothes, as if where he's from in Eastern Europe sleeping along a river isn't out of custom.

I'd always assumed most Battery Park groundskeepers are lesbians (just because they seem so self-contained) but a short brunette stared back beside the wall of pink flowers. Her partner wouldn't stop asking questions. As a rollerblader skirted a family this made the father flail and panic. As I overtook them he stood explaining himself. When a mom stretched both arms to the right her shirt showed sloppy flesh that appealed to me in passing. One man jogged so quietly it was irritating. Afterwards I undid my awkward smile.

Swerving through Kowski Plaza a worker blasted big hexagons clean. Puddles frothed where his hose attached to the hydrant. I got interested in where a zipper slashed

across one woman's hip. I couldn't decide if the Embassy
Suites atrium evoked power or absence. In my ears wind
was a mood and personality. Kristin's apartment reeked of
perfume.

TUESDAY

In the stairwell someone wore my exact same shoes. A white
guy muttered hurrying past. Again I had a hat on. With my
hands stuffed in vest pockets my wrists felt mangled. Kid
sunglasses on the sidewalk glared. Somebody'd dropped a
six-pack of Coronas. I guess I'd expected the glass to be
colored. Beside me a big woman shouted Which bus is
that? In Malcolm X Plaza a boy broke from his wagon,
walked the concrete flowerbed with arms out for balance.
The blank wall caught a pine's morning shadow—8:29.

Near St. Nick's boys yelled What's up with all the
grays? They said Hey girl. An attractive young woman
approached them smiling. Someone descending a ladder
frowned in various directions. Self-knowledge emanating
from a Nigerian teen in two-toned denim convinced me
she was a genius.

A guy leaned against a payphone, using the ledge as
counter for doughnut and coffee. He casually addressed a
passing mom. This came off rude. Still I understood the
desire to seem legitimate.

Spotting front-door Stop Bush signs I envisioned a
family. It was somehow exciting to be on Old Broadway.
At one corner a crossing guard explained So the letter says
this child's already *in* my house. From one sedan's rearview
mirror at least 8 deodorizing trees dangled. The next held

one. A sign spinning from the third read I [heart] Jesus. A grandma's smoldering tights made me think of cardinals. As two women posted flyers I scanned one several back (the least interesting subject: daycare services).

Across 125th a plastic dispenser promoted some college nobody's ever heard of. The slight new possibility I'll have a decent job next year left me fantasizing in terms of real estate. I wanted palatial uptown shabbiness, not the downtown norm. Along a deli a woman making crotch gestures screamed Too bad you're not on top of me now! Passing a cobbler/keymaker's she cried Jamon!

Sidewalk dimmed. Someone exiting what I thought said Methadone Clinic coughed on me. I had to weave through cars where a police station crumbled. Under elevated train tracks a different morning could be felt—urban but not glamorous, and not sordid or schizophrenically commercial either, vaguely religious like floating dust. An Acela train shot past soothing me more than silence would. A sedan backed into garbage bags. A lackadaisical tire store looked neither closed nor open.

Still planning to walk the Hudson I turned south a block early. I guess traffic became an unconscious downer. A pamphlet asked Where was God? across a picture of the World Trade Center exploding. The boldest pages had been printed in Patois.

A French woman winced as I curled up Claremont. A set of buildings I might be able to afford stood fronted by tubes like lifeguard towers. Beyond the lobby someone dug dirt out to his neck. Co-workers tipped a wheelbarrow. They seemed Chilean maybe, very upbeat. When I turned with a double-decker bus the tour guide said something about twenty thousand restaurants. There weren't that many people on board. A gothic address on Union Seminary restored nuance to the day (606 I think).

An old woman locked a church annex labeled Members Only. Another place was called the (something) Lamb Society. Someone explained to his companion: It's like you just made a bed, you know, and now somebody's going to *lie* in it.

As I crossed 112th a boy stood on tiptoe to make his friends laugh; I actually imagined having to kick him in the balls. Under dank blue scaffolds a church's steps looked extra holy. On my own block I held the door for someone exiting the deli. He paused, surprised. Behind me someone impatient exhaled. I had to convince the clerk I knew I'd grabbed plantains (not bananas).

WEDNESDAY

By 8:55 warmth and smells had returned. Double-parked cars made the day feel lived in. An embossed bronze outfit caught my attention. My timing crossing through traffic felt off. I hadn't gone to the bathroom yet though needing to kept me up all night.

Joggers pulled the morning in different directions. A hawk seemed to sway with salsa from a boombox. A local girl walking a ferret grinned like I'd just said something funny. Grass had been aerated. Cylindrical dirt lay next to holes.

The Conservatory Gardens stood closed temporarily. I couldn't tell if temporary meant 10 minutes or a month. Workers beyond the gate sounded relaxed and willfully insular. Hey Shirley one called, I think I found your glasses.

I took a trail to someplace high marked by the Andrew Haswell Green bench. A carved stone praised this first park director and father of New York. These five trees, the engraving read, have been planted in memoriam. I looked around wondering which five they were. I tried not to interrupt one Mexican boy squatting, staring down from his own stillness into the park's. I turned toward a woman riding her bike far below and more listened to the gears than looked.

Across North Meadow signs said BASEBALL FIELDS CLOSED FOR WEATHER OR SERVICE. A gap appeared in one of the fences. Robins glistened and sang all around me. For some reason I was walking painfully slowly, like in dreams where my contacts get way too strong. The far fence rolled back quietly like curtains. I passed handball courts and an ugly trailer.

A sign warned that horse-riders had the right of way. A clump of burrs reminded me of grade school. I stopped under blooming cherry branches. Gazing at petals with a humming inside me I heard girls shout the Pink Panther theme song. I felt paint peeling where my fingers clutched a pole. I tracked couples flickering through trees. When a gull glanced up I said What is there to hope for now?

We stared into the reservoir. The algae beckoned without trying to. One jogger told a friend If he buys both floors your kids should take the top. Another jogger's butt looked tragically bony.

Tennis staff affixed boxes with a puffy machine. A blonde and a Rastafarian exchanged such fierce ground strokes I momentarily respected the rich. Jets arched behind them (watering clay courts). The Rec Center bathroom finally stood propped open. I remembered positive experiences pausing in there.

A gym teacher had set up cones his class was supposed to sprint around. A student 1.6 times taller than the rest looked like some sort of intern. I admitted aloud I'd lost my touch for ignoring problems until each morning walk was complete. But then stepping down a root-laden path I briefly felt like an adroit goat.

Descending a staircase to The Meer I pictured white horses and then one crossed. Students wearing plaid streamed into the Gardens. A chaperone spun around commanding Don't *touch* anything. Don't *do* anything.

I split off towards the Wisteria Pergola. Signs warned 24-Hour Pesticide Spray—parents hold onto children. Two wealthy woman broke branches from a bush. Heart's Delight tulips had fully blossomed. Rose plantings lined the paths, gave an answer to one of my big questions since March: Do flowerbeds hold different bulbs simultaneously, or do species get imported late at night? The plastic pots even had barcodes.

Tears started sliding down my neck. A guard stepping from Lincoln Correctional glared. In the lobby Luis and I mumbled greetings canceled by a closing door.

THURSDAY

Packing up I realized I'd lost my hat, probably yesterday at school. Sparrows fighting over a bagel hunk abruptly abandoned it at 8:54. A van had *Libra* airbrushed with scales beneath. I wondered if I'd always come out on construction scaffolds. I bent and flipped an index card. It was a Things

To Get list—cleaning supplies. But across the front some-one's sneaker left gorgeous treads.

Where I turned up Lenox sidewalk claimed The Sisters Of Sarah Are Coming. Sportcoats from garbage bags lay scattered along the curb. A crossing guard's posse sprawled out on nearby steps. I've often wondered what crossing guards get paid. *Mary Poppins* filled my head again: "Consistent is the Life I Lead." A boy turned and stared while continuing forward clutching his father's jacket.

So many pigeons veered left it felt hard to not follow. A church for sale would make a good co-op. A developer laughed in what had been its front hall. A sexy woman smiled like I'd flattered her. I wondered if I was near the Bill Clinton Library. I pictured an undemanding job, with Bill Clinton liking me.

At 125th one man sold Newports out of a totally con-spicuous white plastic bag. I searched for the Income Tax Assistance Center. A Haitian guy pointed at a stranger's cellphone. A woman guessed He can only mouth words. An optometrist advertised $99 contacts. I made an extra effort to remember this.

When I spotted the tax center the line ran out the door. Families spinning towards me frowned. I continued up Fifth past a stray pink sock and tie-dyes tumbling from a dresser. Window-washers assembling platforms in front of housing projects blanched. Pigeons sorted through a spread of damp Ruffles. Someone punched the D's dot in a doctor's sign. Someone my age passed on an insect-like tricycle. A Puerto Rican flag poked from the seat. The rider tongued a whistle between his lips.

Plaques said Riverbend Candy Store but the closest shop was a deli. On the way past American Storage I wondered where I'll put my stuff this summer. I turned west on 142nd then south on a street called Chisum Place (beside big tow trucks with sirens flashing). Chisum ended and I cut through Delano Village Housing Complex, to the sound of a breezy lawn.

Flags atop City College's cliff flew at half-mast maybe. I couldn't picture a normal flag. Cherries pinked in Fred Samuels Park. Signs hung from trees along an ambiguous house of worship: Prosperity, Salvation, then a blank one, then Bob Marley. Someone told his friend I play the same number every *day*. That's the choice which *saved* my ass. A teacher flinched as though from electric shock. A tossed-out mattress depicted hot air balloons launched from wooden towers. I pushed through a marijuana cloud. Rice spread across sidewalk still held patterns fingers had traced. I wondered if barbers up here could cut white people's hair. I passed the first gay pride flag I'd seen so far north, also a laundromat's free dryers special.

No outdoor line at the tax center now. People emptied pockets and strode through the sensor. I asked a man if I should remove my belt. Everything he said. Then after this was done: Wait, leave the belt. I'd forgotten the pants I wear when walking Uptown have a mostly dysfunctional zipper. It sank as I stepped through the security gate. As I slid the belt through its loops a handsome guard grabbed my bin of metal objects. The next person had arrived. The guard said Keep moving.

FRIDAY

With Kristin's roommate packing up I had to rearrange my schedule. Poaching salmon I listened for thunder. As I stepped out at 11:00 my neck felt strained. When a banker with enormous arm-span gestured from his Gee Whiz Diner booth I flinched, forgetting about the glass between us. Someone with bird-like features stared at me. She twitched her head diagonally. I could easily find her in the largest crowds.

Along Tribeca Wines apartment furnishings stood wrapped with chic brown paper. A Pakistani clerk said something elegant in her phone. A black man mumbled Go fuck yourself. A secretary pointed at the psychedelic burrito hut. This place used to be a blast, she said, I mean *years* ago. I held the door for an overdressed mom on her way into a shop that sold cardboard boxes. I wanted to walk in sun even if it meant extra stop lights. With my gloves still lost I forced my hands in jeans, further harming my wrists. The Sabrett-cart boss called out Good luck you guys. It's blustery.

Near Canal I wondered if calligraphy samples (Ashley, Lauren, Kenneth, Jack) suggest the most popular immigrant names. A pigeon hovered as if reading. A Chinese woman in heels and with zits looked very much alive, part of something greater. Someone opened cellar doors and screamed Hey Nicky!

A tan homeless person surrounded by bags sat on a well-designed staircase chewing something healthy. Men in facemasks hoisted giant bundles—I'd never seen a larger or more chaotic warehouse. I would have sat but the Gourmet Garage bench had just been hosed down. I felt frustrated by a woman's parted hair.

Where I turned up Lafayette lay boxes marked Tuxedo. A Korean man warded off his father's anger. A cab driver didn't want them riding in front. A waitress on her knees wrote out daily specials.

In preparation for clothes shopping (a rarity) I watched how penises bulge based on the cut of pants. As subtle as I thought I was about this some men gave off pretty aggressive signals. Near 12th I passed a church compound filled with magnolia blossoms, thinking Shouldn't I know the names of such places? Someone washed a brass door with the numerals 2-6-5 reflected on his chest. An expensive beauty emulsion center doubled as sandwich café. A woman squatted against movie theater glass with her kitten.

In Union Square two lines of boys beaned each other with tennis balls. A park worker's purple bangs stunned me (sexually). She kept adjusting a sprinkler. A girl in headphones almost got hit as she crossed 18th. From the park someone homeless yelled You fucking blind basketcase! Pigeons climbed from the benches' shadows. Among them I found my legitimate mood. Market lilies bore colors I couldn't have predicted.

Further up Park Ave., approaching Midtown, I wanted to pee without stopping in any of the stores. Having just this sensation on just these blocks recalled a whole previous year of my life. Skinny girls still smoked and complained outside the American Academy of Drama. They stood oblivious of caterers wheeling carts around puddles. An intense Jewish man stared at me, mused on something far away. A plastic dispenser announced Meet America's Poet Laureate! I didn't recognize the person. Polka dots turned on a truck pouring concrete.

Polish girls in lab coats made me cut west. They entered a gourmet deli which for once deserved the title. Through a window I checked out salad stations. The short Guatemalan cashier had a U.S. flag stitched to his pocket. A partially obscured New York Times headline seemed to declare that religion had been imposed on judges.

As I crossed 34th I said hello to Alex, a scholar of Spanish literature, but he had been brooding and could only wave. A woman smiled then snickered like I was snubbing her. A Japanese student covered her mouth from the stairs. It looked dim at first in the library.

...at this temperature streets felt in bloom.

MONDAY

I walked, but had a job interview afterwards so there wasn't time to write about it. I left at 9:14. Two women, one in a wheelchair, took turns reading the Times aloud along the Hudson. A dog stared at its reflection in a fountain basin. An Irish couple stopped to ask when "those cherries" had bloomed (behind, the river sparkled).

TUESDAY

It was the first day in shorts (no keys or cellphone). Raphael had propped the lobby vents. I spun out from Kristin's close to 8:15. Four or five of us hurried past a neon cinema along the river—no one certain how or why this group had formed. The women's sandals seemed fierce and primitive. The saucy mushrooms in a tipped takeout container somehow resisted gravity. The man in front wore a Houston Oilers jersey with 34 and Campbell printed on its back. My mind kept connecting the number to the name.

I noticed that I space crossing intersections—maybe to avoid any consciousness of taxis. Reemerging I felt like part of the sun. A cop showed her ten speed to guys in hardhats. A sign read *Absolutely* No Parking. Moms wearing expensive jeans maintained intense one-on-one connections with kids while chatting just beyond the playground spikes. An older boy fingered through entangled yellow flowers.

Empty barges loomed beneath a little brown aura. I guess I'd missed the haze. Three tall men arched their legs across a rail with each person's shoe pointing out over water. Construction turned part of the path into a tunnel.

On the other side someone Chinese stretched in slacks, pink oxford. A woman rode past doing arm circles.

As two female joggers approached the brunette called Five second break? They kissed. A man slowed down to think and the golf cart behind him also paused. In a restaurant window I saw myself: erratic haircut, stocky quads. Damp grass made me wonder when I'd last seen dew. Someone homeless tossed the final bite of his sandwich overhead to ecstatic gulls.

Curving into Battery Park I watched banana threads gleam against a grandma's chin. I tried not to scatter feasting sparrows. The benches had no backs (as if inviting sleep). A supine Arab couple held each other. A gardener named Jose swore and rattled his shovels. His big hair and earrings kept me conscious of class. Two Staten Island Ferries crossed paths and this was moving like always. A pig-nosed boy asked his mom if she saw the ships. A tipped Dos X's bottle lay with its remaining beer level. At the park's end Brooklyn Heights slid out in terraces and silhouettes.

Turning back beside an Ellis Island ferry I saw one family sat below, frowning, with hundreds of people above them in the morning light. A woman looked up from a New Yorker beaming. Our connection grew so strong I glanced off guilty. A mountain bike stood next to her, reminding me how exotic South Cove once felt. A Russian guy jogged in a v-neck sweater. Two geese sped north just above the Hudson. Two engineers debated how to spread dirt where the Living Memorial to the Holocaust will stand. The v-necked jogger passed again. The Chinese man who'd been stretching passed with sprouting facial moles. A black man stopped to stare at posts present when the river receded. I told him I've often stood watching this.

I smiled at three business people. The more attractive woman said Last night I didn't feel so dumb. The man said You actually weren't all that dumb last night. Plantings crowded the police monument like a chorus on risers. Gaps collected wet pink cherry blossoms.

At a garage I would have waited for the next car to exit but it was a Mercedes so I muttered Fuck you. A Gourmet delivery truck left me disappointed (saran wrap and non-dairy creamers).

I wondered if stencils along a corporate Asian restaurant really said anything. I wondered if a Verizon truck's Kerry/Edwards sticker violated company policy. Taped to the back window hung a tabloid 9-11 spread: Lest We Forget. Sawed-off pipes in the middle of the road left me wondering what had been there before. A boxy car's side read *P.R.CRUISIN*. A bald woman sipped coffee.

WEDNESDAY

By the time I finished tax corrections it was almost eighty degrees. I experimented with the watch I'd found in our recycling room. At 11:19 it dangled from my wrist. Further up my arm it looked funny. With Frankie holding the elevator I hurried down the hall. Mr. Menon (the landlord) said Hello? as I squeezed past boxes.

As I exited one woman sensed she was only wearing a long brown sweater and clogs. She tugged the sweater's waistband further down her thighs. Rice lay in the path's cracked tiles. An abandoned stroller made me swerve.

On 114th I crossed a construction lot, wishing it could stay forever sandy. Amid plywood a boombox let out rhythmic moans. A worker drank juice from a foil-wrapped jug. Another held his partner's ladder and smoked while sifting through keys. Buckets crashed overhead. My neck scrunched. Tennis shoes dangled from the nearest wires.

I gave up the plan to walk Riverside Park since at this temperature streets felt in bloom. A Puerto Rican girl more than met my stare. A man carrying his laundry in garbage bags held on as seams showed. The front flap of a woman's skirt fetishized the zipper. Botanica's clerk rinsed his mug with bottled water. Petals drifted from tall podiums where he assembled bouquets.

I glanced toward a barber's looking for men but instead found reflected Heineken bottles. Someone in a short-sleeve oxford sneezed four times then blew his nose. An empty Peter Pan bus passed with a martial arts movie playing. A late-blossoming cherry branch reflected off the bus's tinted rear. Inside a Victoria's Secret shopping bag I noticed albums (records) and a paperback book. Victoria's Secret bags must be sturdiest.

A Baptist congregation declared itself the friendliest church in town. It advertised a film called Climax 2. Trellises along the youth hostel made me want to cry. I'd stayed there in the 90s. A guy with his wheelchair perched against a project wall strained smiling back. I guess he preferred being the one to look. Then there was a soothing row of geraniums.

A soccer field's dimensions puzzled me until I realized it ran one city block. When I checked the time my watch's second-hand jerked. When I jiggled my wrist the second-hand sank. Crossing 96th I slipped off the watch. Somebody with a cane carried wads of tissue. Someone hauling shovels wore a shirt with Ready Willing and Able printed down the back. A dumpling restaurant's sign announced A Place of Balance (the phrase appealed to me). A dim store sold used desks starting at $210. Who would ever buy one?

From the glaring heat I coveted two businessmen's samosas. It felt good to pass papayas and Haitian mangoes. Two Dominican guys screamed Hey! into a crowd and somehow the right girl looked up. A separate girl thrust her hips sexually and screeched in people's faces. A British girl answered her mother's question: *Love* you, mummy. I *love* you.

Amid Frederick Douglass homes it became clear a lot of boys will wear long white t-shirts this summer. Strangers called out from paths and benches. The lawns had somehow already dried beige. The day turned sultry as I reached Columbus. An idling sky-blue truck restored me. So did two Jamaican sisters giggling about the concept latchkey kid. At 110th and Lenox a lady bent huffing. Her companion glanced off unconcerned.

THURSDAY

The bottom stairs had been lined with velcro strips. The lobby radio played Rod Stewart's "Young Turks." At 8:24 sticky stuff from trees lay sprinkled across the tops of cars. Fragrant air swept along a block of transparent garbage bags. A frenzied sparrow stuck its beak through a feather and muzzled itself. With his first step in the park one boy lit a cigarette. I tucked my hands into sweater sleeves. Informed-looking women carried umbrellas.

Birds called from rushes, black with blues heads— everyone else probably knows their names. A woman tore bagels then receded behind branches. Sparrows held their ground against a couple seagulls. A frizzy grackle staggered about as if blind.

Cones blocking the Mumford Gate caused me to cringe. But it was just two tiles getting patched. A flyer affixed to the wheelchair-entrance announced The Gardens will be closed Wednesday May 4th due to our annual Fundraiser Gala. Thunberg Spiraea (I'd grabbed a new *Garden Highlights*) had sprung up silver. The plaque on one bench declared Happy 50th Birthday Billy! Another decreed Enjoy this bench with a kind man. Enjoy this day because you can.

Someone sprawled on his stomach photographing hyacinths. After an initial shock it seemed soothing and appropriate that someone bitchy oversaw the Garden staff. *Act*ually, she told a Caribbean man, You're going to *scrub* this wall. Behind them someone with long blond hair meditated as if you had to look like him to meditate. All my favorite narcissi had bloomed: Soft Belle, Minnow, Trevithian. Generally this was the reign of narcissi: Jack Snipe, Jetfire, Spellbinder, Jubilee. I couldn't tell which tulips would open as soon as morning sun hit. The creamy Alfred Heinekens stood ready. Some of the Texel Blues did also. Heart's Delights looked smeared, jagged. Magnolia petals overflowed the path. Somebody Muslim and I smiled then she sat with a frown. Surrounding pink made me want to sleep.

At 104th I watched a sexy teacher slip through yellow Caution tape. She tried the Children's Center lobby entrance. A policeman delicately let this pass. A chauffeur snapped two fingers so fast I couldn't separate myself from the sound. A white boy hopped in place to adjust his bladder. He didn't care about looking gay and I envied how physically present this made him.

Nurses near 100th St. greeted each other warmly. It didn't seem to matter if they'd never met. A spaniel's serious jogging face resembled its master's. A deli trapdoor rippled like roots under concrete. I would have scanned the top New York Times but there were coins spread to hold the stack down. I wondered if a guy in camouflage was aware right now we're occupying countries. Gadget stores displayed the newest AC models and fans.

Pedestrians crowded in a box of sun between curb and the reach of the widest cars. Someone getting used to a cane never let it touch sidewalk. I spaced out along Park Ave. imagining insulting Antonin Scalia.

Back on Madison a boy broke from his father, finished the trip to school by himself. Back on Fifth the Gardens' gate reminded me of sliding living-room doors. Friendly Café now sold fresh orange-carrot-apple juice hybrids. A scruffy cyclist carrying a backpack became a cop with walkie-talkie. Someone my age in a fedora made me think Haberdashery. Sun dusted light under The Meer's surface allowed me to both look and think.

Curling into Lenox Street Deli I crashed against a woman's arm. I'd misjudged her breadth. (As always) it was impossible to tell which customers really stood in line. People scratched lottery tickets along both counters. An impatient Indian mom came off looking rude. A slow-eyed cashier beckoned me forwards. Her kindly gesture to indicate Do you want a shopping bag? made me secretly commit to coming back.

FRIDAY

I hovered outside the kitchen curious if Yuki takes her orals this afternoon. On our landing I could barely squeeze past a crib. A barefoot grandma brushed her teeth. A cute Puerto Rican girl chewing a wad of gum spoke walkie-talkie style like she was frenching her phone. Coil and gauze facemasks lay just beyond the lobby. I'd guess this happened about 8:45.

In the park I noticed I was still half asleep, staring at a muddy path, thinking of how alienated we all must be politically. On a footbridge in The Ravine I stopped and listened. Bird songs kept seeming to build momentum. I understood Wagner a little better. A collie split off and strayed beyond the fence but knew what to do when its owners called. A woman clearing branches buttoned hi-tech gloves.

A fiftyish couple hauled farmer's market bags to a housing complex on W. 99th. The man cinched a support strap around his waist. I didn't ever want to live in any other city. A Guatemalan boy's gaudy leather jacket spelled out New York in Gothic font. Penguins dangled from his parents' rearview mirror. Pink cherries amid Frederick Douglass Homes got cancelled by ugly architecture.

As he passed someone with dreads began speaking aloud (I think just to diffuse his inner tension). On Broadway melted cars leaned diagonally along a police station. An Ace Hardware advertised $64.99 Passover Kettles. A Piggyback construction vehicle bore down on me in reverse. I kept drifting further out towards traffic. Finally the driver noticed and waved.

A girl said That's *great* but I need *your* love. A mom asked in a stroller How do Jason and Jackson start? A voice cried back J and G! A disassembled grocery store was just cubic space cut by shelving. An Italian restaurant's signboard read GOD BLESS AMERICA, twice. Somebody'd left out a pair of spray-painted gold Adidas.

Inside Gourmet Garage I gave up stealing currant scones once I saw they were sugar coated. In line someone young and healthy rode a slender scooter/wheelchair hybrid. His content demeanor fit 9:25. I turned down a grocery bag then asked the cashier for one. That's what I thought, she said, You don't want somebody mugging you for the cheese. It was true—I'd walked all this way for some affordable Irish cheddar.

Passing newsstands I wondered why Big Energy needs tax breaks. A laundromat displayed stuffed animals: Snoopy as the Red Baron and a wrinkled pug. One falafel place appeared fanciest. Cooks scanned the Times at its outdoor table. I peeked under a deli flap hoping to learn the names of late spring flowers. But nothing they sold was blooming in New York. The Cuban clerk nodded like he understood.

Old men asked specifically for quarters. One pushed TVs in a laundry cart. One Polish mom pushing a carriage looked my way with a sexualized jolt. One Gay City News headline about the pope-elect claimed No Benediction (Dark Days to Come). Under one tall attractive woman I felt like a pauper.

Twin sisters stuck bouquets in the Isadora and Ida Duncan statue. Surrounding tulips maybe would open today. As a butcher crossed, coins spilled from his pocket. Squatting he found a pencil that he liked. I avoided stepping on Winnie the Pooh's face although this was just a Dixie cup. A twitching man spoke into his fist: Over here, we have the *star*let's house…

A boy wearing a yarmulke said in his phone I'd hear you better if you didn't scream. The mother and daughter I talked with on Election Day passed like total strangers. The hyacinth poking through chicken-wire resembled white asparagus. A leaky hose in front of a doctor's office sprayed several pedestrians. Somehow they never saw it coming. For some reason Luis got paternalistic in the stairwell, making sure his tools didn't trip me up.

People about to collapse (emotionally) must often stand beneath.

MONDAY

At 9:00 Kristin's front hall smelled like lilies. A woman wrapped a silk scarf around her ears. The reedy Taiwanese girl followed her dad, stroking her scooter forwards. Crossing Church I sensed this one skyline image gradually replacing most childhood memories.

Wine we'd drunk to celebrate Kristin staying in New York left me scattered. Delivery-cart tracks rolled in and out of puddles. At the end somebody stacked soda cases. City Hall reflected in the deep blue part of windshields. Giant light bulbs had duct tape at their tops. A driver slept with his mouth agape, looking like a Francis Bacon. A twelve-year-old with an earring tilted his head and stared.

A Canadian trucker's gap-toothed smile reminded me I'd dreamt of kissing pink cotton. I remembered another dream (hiding long fingernails; then a cavernous house my mom had rented, with pink confetti in the front bushes).

On E. Broadway a monk wearing saffron robes peered out from his storefront temple. He seemed impatient. Several nearby institutions had titles approximating World Center for Buddhist Thought. Somebody androgynous with feet propped on garbage bags cooed. Someone's boss watched storefront gates rise. In the Wing Yung Public School window kids' names hung posted to sheep and swans. Generators lit a fruit market's lamps. I passed the Confucius statue, considering the other statue—in Chatham Square, dedicated to the first anti-drug advocate in China—puzzled by this entire history, presuming we'd forced opium on a lot of people.

Climbing the Manhattan Bridge I saw carts canted toward the curb. Behind a power box two bodies lay zipped in rainbow sleeping bags. A pink cherry below on

Bayard lost none of its charm beside ugly municipal buildings. Division remained the most "real" street I'd ever seen in New York—what was it, the dimensions? How a figure's always cutting diagonally across?

The closest roof prompted further questions: Do taggers just lean and paint downwards? I felt like I'd read a lot lately about the specific political roots of graffiti. Where I stepped somebody had written RACECAR. The next patch said Consider: 4 % of Chinese are registered to vote. A sleek silver D-train ascended.

Laundry hanging in sixth-floor kitchens could have signified economic ingenuity or despair. I passed my ex-girlfriend Abby's building trying to guess which room was hers. A Q-train shot by next to me. Fences on both sides shuddered. I kept withdrawing, away from the cold, petrifying like some disappointed reptile. Water taxis took forever to disappear. Waves blowing northeast spiraled sometimes. While spray crashed over Pearl Street's rocks someone who looked like me took photographs. Cobblestones turned vivid as somebody crossed. Dumbo's office-lofts stood solid.

Fences corralled me to Sands and Jay. Brooklyn felt even colder than the bridge. I grew frustrated behind construction vehicles. I got lost in an endless courtyard filled with crown-like tulips resembling Westpoints. Further up Tillary I found a Brooklyn Bridge entrance. One boy passed with cornrows, driving jauntily but clutching a tissue wad. A well-scrubbed cop eyed my hood skeptically. A strip of dry leaves swirled like a dragon.

The Jehovah's Witnesses clock's flashing spaced me out. Staten Island seemed hilly and half-covered in shade. I wanted to ask one woman if she needed help (though economically she looked fine). The song "Candy" by the band Cameo emerged from my past to overwhelm most of this bridge crossing. Everyone spoke Italian and paused erratically. My ears clogged to the point where two congestions touched.

Along Park I read about the Senate leader's fiery speech to some church of 10,000. "We Got the Beat" drifted from an adjacent bar. On my walk back to the elevators Raphael ducked behind his desk (delighting some kids). On the ride up I considered how nothing irritates me more than getting arrested by an infant's gaze. I'd taken my pants off before the door had closed, needing my legs to rub gentle air. I had to run warm water on both hands before I could write anything.

TUESDAY

I didn't put contacts in because of blotchy corneas. The blossoms beyond my glasses resembled distant snowcapped mountains. From the example of a bald man squatting under a bus-stop sign I projected everyone embracing today with a casualness I lacked. So I turned around amid the acoustical preface to "Hotel California." My apartment felt like refuge from a punishing sun. I put in my contacts and, with one eye pulsing, passed from Don Henley's voice to 8:37 brightness. Luis glanced up from his tools. He ignored my nod. Heavy traffic held me at the curb just long enough to generate penned-in hysteria.

In the park a woman kept saying "turtle" as she spoke of bygone springs spent with a brother. I wondered what response she so craved from her boyfriend. Crabapple boughs (a guess) bloomed out from the general green. The Meer lay glassy. My neighbor with a wheelchair and beret passed slowly, so his dog could piss before the leash went taut. A gangly girl smiled to confirm the sad respect we shared for this elder. A redwing blackbird spun displaying its stripes. A heron poking along the water's edge slalomed through reeds whenever possible.

Out of shoulder-deep muck stepped a normal pigeon; it climbed ashore and shook off. A woman performing knee bends looked confused. Approaching obnoxious boys I blanked. Willows had dropped fuzzy wormy strands. An old ashen beech twinkled.

Inside the Gardens a squirrel broke a branch and sniffed. The Untermeyer Fountain was flowing again. A young gay white guy in heavy-framed glasses led five tough teens around the blandest tulips. A student whispered That's the lady from the office. Where she pointed a woman did tricep-building push-ups. Benches bearing Freshly Painted signs resembled dark horses with glossy coats. Mist among magnolias inspired me to pass through gardeners' sprays. As I turned in I found figures wearing facemasks and full body-suits. Orange lamplight glowed under thickening branches.

I exited surrounded by wiry women with powder-blue sweatshirts that said Volunteer. Late-blooming narcissi pleased me most: Pixit, Jenny, Lemondrops. Jewel of Spring tulips contained all I'd ever wanted (like Morning Glory muffins). Those Virginia Bluebells, someone said, will be gone before you know. The trucks roaring down Fifth sounded like a fantasy. The lilacs explained my itchy pupils.

A pony-tailed photographer said Hi from where he lay on slabs, sounded kind and real—made the sixties seem a country people still could visit from. Police vans made the trail I climbed a squeeze. Near the compost heap one shady mound turned into a man awakening with stubble. Birders exchanged binoculars, consistently dressed in long dark coats. From Rustic Bridge #32 I watched a Raisinettes box glisten. The pulled weeds looked like watercress.

The waterfall just past Huddlestone Arch deserves sustained attention. People about to collapse (emotionally) must often stand beneath. Sunbeams rippled against thick stalks. I wanted to compliment the broken glass. A bicyclist hit stairs, veered toward dirt, partially spinning onto Park Drive traffic. The lingering puddles in Lasker Rink would dry this afternoon.

A turtle stretched its neck farther than I thought possible. I told a swan There's watery light reflecting off your belly. One smiling fat man propped his head on the thinnest of papers (AM News). One Asian man did bizarre torso twists and two white girls mimicked his routine.

Amid fluorescent light in Parkview Deli I sensed how much other mornings differed from mine. As a carpenter strained to recall coworkers' requests the sandwich-girl's thigh pulsed. A deliveryman spun about desperate for somebody to sign his invoice. A Mexican boy in a cowboy hat made hauling a guitar seem easy. An African woman strode south with blue laundry bags on her head. My left eye had pinked slightly. My right one held a dead bug.

WEDNESDAY

Klever (the ex-doorman) sat back behind the desk for a day, so I stopped and we discussed his kids. I didn't check my cellphone on the way out because I didn't want Klever to think I hadn't enjoyed our talk. But when I got to Church it was 12:21. Leaving at lunch hour left me dizzy. My grandpa's blue raincoat sealed most pores. I sensed why painted bodies die. I noticed the distinct shape of every building. It felt like flickers of consciousness around my family.

By Reade I'd turned woozy—passing a Bento Box cart covered in Grand Opening signs, then caught between a rottweiler and an aggressive cocker spaniel. Someone screamed at the spaniel's owner Move! Walk away! I'm trying, the woman said, I don't know what's *happening*!

The situation dissolved except lingering stares. A boy appeared in ersatz medieval armor, tapped his sword every second step. A tired woman glared back like I'd checked her out (but I only started looking once she checked out me). Plum branches bloomed along a parking garage.

Still adjusting to humidity I almost caused a crash at the complicated Park Row intersection. A Fung Wah bus driver stood stiff wearing sunglasses. An old Chinese man seemed to sense how stylish his brown bell-bottoms were. Across the street both stores sold bulletproof vests; I can't believe cops aren't given that stuff.

I cut towards the McDonald's off Bowery, desperate for a bathroom, pessimistic about my chances. Maudlin flute music played inside. Bland woodblock prints and ferns surrounded a two-floor fountain. Appraising angular lamps on my push upstairs I wondered if the Asian theme targeted tourists or locals. I was the only white person in the place. I would have told a line of girls the men's room sat empty but didn't know if this might come across as insulting. I left feeling soothed.

Mott St.'s charming vertical signs mitigated my return to weird air-pressure. I swerved onto Aldrich past a long austere post office. A stylist dried salon windows with just an index card. A bike lay curled and melted. I could hear my heart beat for about a block. Then I was back on Bowery, watching pairs of women sift through rhinestones.

As always when I'm in a rush downtown I passed a sandwich shop that looked appealing. With a pulley-system someone dropped planks through an apartment window (no sound). With a tiny broom a custodian steered hissing water along the curb. Somebody else wrapped a deli display-case in blue plastic. Someone wiped the demonstration slicer he had whirring on the sidewalk. I wondered why everything in restaurant-supply stores looks dusty. A white truck double-turning (does that make sense?) stripped the fender off an old black woman's sedan. Pedestrians winced.

Potted geraniums along the Bowery Bar wall left me worried rowdy people would push them over. Pint glasses glared from a stoplight box. The cab of a UPS truck looked breezy. A rotund man walked as if each step was a cringe. Rosary beads? he mumbled. I sensed but somehow never saw necklaces on a hanger. I stopped to watch kids play soccer with a green fuzzy size-4 ball. I wondered why workers' gloves often have the palm dyed dripping red. What had seemed a taxi flashed sirens—made everyone pull to the curb.

As we approached Union Square perfume off one white woman's fringe left me feeling passive. In James Madison Park teens slept sitting with dark cloth tied around their face. Behind them various newspapers had been hung to dry. Behind this stood a pine oak from James Madison's yard. Close to it a boy bit into something pink.

Somebody stared down a cab about to cut him off and I smiled because I'm often that person. Somebody sticking his head from a van tucked it back in like I'd wanted to kiss him. When I dropped a quarter one man leapt as if to prove he wasn't stealing. Standing straight I almost collided with a couple. Amid a jostling crowd as the walk sign changed I couldn't really see.

THURSDAY

Pale mist at 9:03 felt like my natural weather. I wondered if my hair looks best foggy mornings. I glanced back and saw Frankie wearing goggles. Hello, he called, instead of his usual OK!

Honking geese made the morning lucid and tender. Dandelions hadn't been there Tuesday. A West African dad curling dumbbells spoke to his daughter in the prettiest French. A jogger in a coolie hat barely moved forwards. I turned into the North Woods just as three gay Germans (two shaved bald) stepped out. An hour later I'd see them in the East 100s.

As I ascended toward greenness two white-bellied birds I'd thought were blue jays sang. Though Thoreau stresses being still in the woods I couldn't sit and wait for rustlings to reveal their sources. After more bad job news and predawn insomnia I wanted to know this world with me walking through it. A man with dreads drinking coffee and I kept weaving past each other on divergent trails. A worker stood on woodchips, placing calls. I crossed two bridges that don't get named in the 150th Anniversary Map and Guide but iron grids directing The Loch somehow spoke to all that history.

Climbing loose rock into North Meadow I came out on three kids and a baseball diamond. The two boys sat silent in orange sweatshirts with numbers. The blond girl in glasses giggled looking up. A guy bounced near handball courts, waiting for a game.

I passed two mutts really going at it—the owners talking politely as if someplace else. The top dog got pulled when a Parks Enforcement vehicle approached. Two officers stepped out. The bottom-dog's owner apologized for removing its leash. I'm sorry, she said, I just thought with all this space. I'm sorry, I kept hearing, but I could only see the police truck. I'm sorry I'm sorry.

The East Meadow lay almost absent of dogs. I couldn't tolerate one airedale's master's strides. Planners assembling a stage at the park's edge stood split along a giant extension cord. From the Fifth Ave. wall someone watched with a frown. It was obvious he wanted work.

The billowing outfit of the woman stepping from a bus somehow never obscured her pleasant shape. Our paths met at the Arthur Brisbane memorial. Brisbane sounded familiar, but the overwrought catalogue of his achievements suggested a gulf between now and 1936. A doorman and a poodle jogged past with both appearing to do it for the other's health.

In the Gardens plaid-skirted girls with Spencer sweatshirts sat on tiles sketching Texel Blues. Queen of the Nights and Esthers looked promising (though my walks never are timed right for tulips). The Actaea narcissus finally showed itself lovely. New staff taking notes followed a barrel chested trainer. More Star Magnolias, she said. You saw a lot of them in Queens.

Beyond the gates boys rode bikes and gnawed at Good Humor ice cream, mostly King Cones. A furtive Peruvian adjusted his fishing rod. Across The Meer I saw Luis—or someone of similar proportions and in the same ribbed shirt—stretch his calves. I'd never thought of Luis as a jogger.

Exhausted ladies laughed outside La Hermosa. They didn't seem all that religious but definitely had entered a protective space. A double-decker bus cruised past labeled North Loop: Harlem/Museum Mile/Park. A futon frame slipped from a garbage man's shoulder. I've always found garbage-truck rhythm soothing. Trophies propped a window on W 112th. One showed a football player get tackled. Another vertically spelled out SCIENCE. In the next room a rustic frog troupe played banjos: this I think was Senegalese.

In Family Horizons cups stood marked with kid's names and bean types. Ribbons flapped in front of Martin Luther King Jr. Senior Citizens' Center. On the next block a baseball diamond lay overrun with weeds. A bumper sticker read Born with nothing... and I've *still* got it! A senior-citizen van decomposed. A woman waited with crossed arms while a bus scooped her wheelchair.

FRIDAY

None of the clothes I'd washed in the sink had dried. I had to put back on what I'd worn before showering. Someone trailed me on the way downstairs. She hurried past the mailboxes. It turned out she had a bus to catch and she sprinted in front of it, the way I will, holding it in place. I nodded at where Luis squatted beside a wheelbarrow.

Along The Meer a girl flinched each time she brought her cigarette close. As I passed the playground I was thinking whoever fired my brother must be a total prick, hoping my mom felt no whiplash after getting rear-ended last night, wondering if I've strayed too far from grounded pessimism or I'm just less afraid of failure.

My trail sank beneath the 110th St. Bridge. I'd wanted to continue west but felt reluctant to turn while a foppish black man and German shepherd approached. This stranger's Good morning was classy and kind. One stray daffodil got me thinking Shouldn't I love this? Isn't this what I am? But it grew boring to be so metaphoric.

Along 108th I understood why businesses include that street in their titles. It seemed the perfect distance from crowded blocks. A woman sprayed blue mist and wiped gunk from her dashboard. From one rearview mirror dangled mini Puerto Rican boxing gloves. From the next hung a Native American hoop. On the Southern Baptist church—with its name set perpendicular to form a cross at the T's—a taped-up sign just read Cuidado. Two girls sat in the front of a red sedan reading thick books, using bookmarks.

I passed pastry shops I would have tried by now if the neighborhood didn't get so sketchy at night. Watching deliverymen I wondered why people spit. Where I turned into Riverside Park someone who looked just like my friend Mike Yusko sat smoking, grinning—just as Mike would if he woke up this early. I glanced his way assuming he'd acknowledge me first, since it's easy to recognize somebody walking. Below us the city had recently installed a triceratops and tyrannosaurus you could climb. Pink cherry blossoms lined the promenade (I knew I'd never pass under them).

A townhouse I otherwise appreciated held patriotic ribbons wrapped around the porch. A dog crossed with its owner calling Stephen, wait! Two scottish terriers looked less intelligent side-by-side. An old Japanese woman wore a bowler hat. The question Was she attractive? made no sense. *I* was attracted to her. She needed my gaze and I delivered it.

Around New Moon Bakery it became clear that my gay side went for guys losing hair color, sporting metallic tones, with refined but somewhat stodgy taste in music. In front of a deli I learned one hundred days of the new Bush presidency had passed. One cellphone place also specialized in "sexy tongue rings" and, considering a photo from the movie *Thirteen*, I thought about how sexy they truly are, except when they make someone lisp, but even that's sometimes especially sexy. One bike-shop display presented women pulling at bikini bottoms. I couldn't tell if New York was a sensual city.

From under a cab poked a pizza box printed with dewy tomatoes. Tony Alamo Christian Ministries left imitation newspapers on select windshields. The headlines read Flood. My eyes followed one fire escape to a flock of Happy 5th Birthday balloons. I wondered if that's a big deal in Dominican culture. As someone wearing a puffy jacket performed Tai Chi on her building's lawn I wondered how much of it was psychological. I felt like I move so much more than her while stretching.

Accelerating down 109th I fell in with a group approaching the B–C entrance. It seemed I was about to board a train. Concrete slabs twirled high above. A construction worker spoke casually with a friend while walking across a pit on a beam. Someone carrying a child chipped soccer balls over the playground fence. The defter he dribbled the more desperate it got.

Two cooks and one distracted woman made an intense triangle. How's six thirty? the meek white guy said. *Please* let me think, the woman replied, now do you have a dollar?

On my own block I passed Slavs staring out from a truck platform, pointing and leering into the park. I kept waiting for them to say something so the moment could feel complete. Passing Frankie felt so repetitive I didn't care how nice he was. I whined about our hallway reeking of incense. Sifting through stray envelopes I forgot which mail I wanted.

I had to approach a cop for Manhattan Bridge directions.

MONDAY

After a night of bad sleep in uncomfortable boxers I stepped out to puffy repetitive sounds. A high-pitched drill at 8:02 gave me giddy pleasure. I'd clipped my toenails and liked how they now itched. I couldn't pay attention to certain streets anymore (like Chambers). In a dry cleaner's window a fan had rusted but never stopped spinning. As I curved along the last bearable stretch of Broadway someone handed me a complimentary Wall Street Journal. He took the paper back with a bow. It became a fun exchange.

All around City Hall people turned to smile at tulips they were passing. Wind had pulled a tabloid apart so that separate sheets fluttered across the lawn. I considered how butts hang nonexistent in current expensive jeans—how I'd almost been taken in by that. I approached a phalanx of women at the bottom of Foley Square. They glided through a sequence of postures. Radios blasted martial music. It might have had to do with the Falun Gong.

Police led someone through a battered gate. The handcuffed guy asked his nearest escort How many cops in a building like this? She answered with a tone too soft to grasp. Where they once stood a guard's salami sandwich glistened. Rippling blue construction plastic made it hard to face Columbus Park.

Plastic sleeves on fishmongers suggested flotation devices. The backs of fish marts resembled insurance offices: plywood desks, tacky paintings and fixtures. Melons looked luscious crammed in boxes.

North on Grand I followed one woman really tuned-in to all the blinking lights. Beside a going out of business 99 cents store somebody stopped sweeping the curb to think. A coworker consolidated styrofoam scraps.

Another unscrewed the standpipe and shoved up it a giant rod.

Men paced Sara D. Roosevelt Park. There was a $20 flat rate to Foxwoods Casino or a $70 package with 52 in chips. A sunburned boy left his bike unlocked along a pharmacy. My breath tightened. A woman stepped from Kossar's Bialys making almost indetectable progress. Stretch-pant stirrups clung at her ankles.

At Clinton somebody my age in seagreen cords flung her head, convinced I was following. There was nowhere to turn. The moment grew stale. Parking meter shadows lay stark and clean. An old man bulged his eyes from the exact edge of a project's yard. I thought I heard velcro.

Dropping down Broom I saw Chinese phonecard-saleswomen had a more professional air than clerks behind counters. They dressed a lot like stewardesses. Exercise troupes packed handball courts. One extended its motions with pocket fans. One old woman did knee squats. Others marched in place, arched their hips (everybody discrete as in a Balthus painting).

Beyond Canal two boys hoisted a rumbling metal sheet. A double-length bus blocked the crosswalk with me staring at its black accordion hinge. A Mohegan Sun agent hugged her clipboard: taxed, but respectful of elders. Storefront temples stood well-rubbed and soothing. Someone straightened his mask beneath bifocals.

Exercises continued in Foley Square. The rear of a UPS truck held so many more boxes than expected but still wasn't that well organized. City Hall Park looked Southern, pink. At the one-man carwash Armor All and Windex dangled from rims of garbage cans. Just noticing made my pupils scratchy.

In the lobby Raphael seemed extra warm. He was training a block-shaped man to sit behind the desk. Picking up on this person's shyness I pressed my key against elevator buttons. Kristin exited reading a script. Man am I late! she said—kissing me, hurrying out.

TUESDAY

People hurried by with their hands in sleeves (8:35). I'd left my hat at Kristin's. For once I could picture setting it down (beside the table with the phone). But our hemisphere had tilted toward the sun and there was room for dressing errors.

I crossed into the park heading straight for The Meer where a giant silver bird stood at its center like a bubble. The bird's charcoal beak resembled a sickle. Lodged branches swayed near the surface and I crouched, happy to be drawn there. A Saab followed pedestrian paths after turning from Park Drive five feet too soon. No one made much effort to get out of its way. Sparrows shuddered in fence slots. Squirrels finally looked trim. Friendly Snack Bar's salesman hosed the front tiles.

I wound through party-planning supplies and trucks parked along The Meer's edge. With somebody jogging laps around the Gardens it felt I too was huffing. Pink-striped Dreamland tulips (thousands) shook set off by thin swatches of Blue Aimables. Two cordial women appeared to have forgotten each other's names. Both alleés had been converted into taut, glamorous tent corridors. Volunteers bugged the real boss for assignments. The Peer Gynts had their moment as pinkest bloom. The South Beds still held a lot of withered narcissi. Amid an expansive electric buzz I saw the Burnett Fountain flowing.

I wandered east across lumpy grass. I really needed to cover my hands but pockets hurt my damaged wrists. It seemed impossible that until this spring I'd never walked the park before noon. Curving with damp rock swells provided the day's most distinct impression (by far). I didn't know it then. This is something I should learn to recognize.

In the East Meadow samoyeds stood fixating on their master. It was mostly spry couples in light spring jackets. Someone calling in a stock order smiled apologetically. Two chirping robins bumped chests.

Veering towards The Loch one Russian went from cooing at his infant son to whipping his mild dog with a leash. This sweet labrador looked gray around the edges. Great Hill lay bare except for a busty baby-boomer throwing her retriever a stick as she climbed, smiling behind sunglasses. Through branches I glimpsed clear blue sky. A group of twenty birders approached—all dressed from catalogues. I wondered if I'll end up a birder.

I had to wait for the distracted nineteen-year-old to drop his orange construction flag before I could cross 110th. Inside Organic Forever a pianistic, aromatic morning passed. At the counter an Aussi explained why banks sometimes want extra collateral. The Bangladeshi clerk caught on quickly, anticipating each sentence's conclusion, weighing my almonds without looking down. Back on Frederick Douglass someone sniffing in his shirt shouted Big guy. But a dollar?

Just as I began promising myself No more than a glance at Morningside Park I came upon its waterfall. A basketball spun where water dropped. A park worker muttered, making me feel white. Geese opened their eyes but didn't untuck bills when I passed, except for one still dreaming.

From 116th I read African menus, trying to remember which place I'd heard so much about. I think it was Nice and Easy. It seemed shady interiors (not bright windows) were a virtue up here. One tour-bus driver waited out the stoplight leaning forward with his chin on a fist. One carpenter carrying cement-mix bags took quick but delicate steps. I wondered if the Shabbazz family owned the faux mosque at 116th (and really had been charitable as posters claimed). I wondered how it's decided which deli people hang out in front of and if there are times when a deli needs this. Gazing up I wanted to inhabit a room with curvy walls again.

Flyers on a neighboring scaffold said This Is What They Will Do, showed blueprints for a "mountain of million dollar towers stuck between you and the park." I didn't doubt it. Re-entering the courtyard I noticed all the signs hung like we have a security system. Only from the stairs would I admit today I had to talk with Mr. Menon about August rentals. I turned back down then froze. I stepped and paused—since when so indecisive?

WEDNESDAY

I couldn't put in contacts right away with Kristin getting ready for work. Judging from postures of people out the window warm temperatures were back. Finally I heard my love finish at the sink and sort through papers. I stepped from the building at 9:06. A boy kept sobbing but trying to sound mad. I *hate* you! he told his younger brother. *You* made the mess and I *cleaned* up everything! A passing woman with white pants made it suddenly the season for that color. A hunched figure filled the crosswalk as a Don't Walk sign flashed solid. There was nothing to do but deftly swing around her.

At City Hall Park a postcard rack got me thinking about my grandparents. An iron grid got pushed towards me by a construction guy with a blind spot. I wanted to know the fountain's name. I craved New York proper nouns. I need to develop a place-remembering technique—the way I'll hold onto numbers until I find a pen.

Climbing the Brooklyn Bridge beside a clover-leaf entrance I felt like one of the people in cars. I sensed some strange disclosure coming as an architect talked on her business line. I knew I was watching a Kennedy-class ferry dock at Whitehall Station. I knew Governor's Island. I didn't know what to call the silvery bridge cables. I wondered which cyclists would slip into loafers in bathrooms outside their offices.

I opted for the shortcut exit (a staircase). An unmarked police car blocked Red Cross Drive. The officer never glanced up from his book as I passed. Skirting Concerto tulips beneath the BQE I paused along Walt Whitman Square. Even listening to one sexy clerk's heels clack across the plaza felt a little glum. I wished to have known this borough center before the 1897 consolidation.

A short florist nodded then froze and looked glazed. Construction pushed me out into traffic. I had to approach a cop for Manhattan Bridge directions. I prepared for him to just squint at me. Go back to Jay take the south ramp he said (but he was kind). There's no pedestrian path on the north side? I pressed. This seemed frustrating, since one point of the walk had been to look for Williamsburg around the river bend.

One townhouse glared among blocks of industry (I pictured what it was like living there). I followed an irritating network of Keep Out fences to where a sign said Bikers Use North Path. Crossing back under the bridge I'd somehow started ascending the side I wanted, curving on the way up, smiling at a woman coasting past in cowboy boots. Her belly glowed beyond the button-down shirt. Below someone weed-whacked through crumbling lots.

A flickering bedspread made it clear one abandoned bank was inhabited. Storm clouds came on cool drafts but close by millions of wave tips sparkled. Water slipped onto chocolaty beaches toward which I felt emotionally distant. The East River had no obvious current: spontaneous whitecaps, slick or fluttery stretches. The four impotent smokestacks near Vinegar Hill obscure far more mini-turrets emitting fumes. Sections of the Navy Yard smoldered. Beyond Domino Sugar I saw the humble warehouse where I'd lived for years. I remembered how glad I once got above it in final descent from Milwaukee.

A perfect crescent moon had been smashed out of a window. On a nearer windowsill a pigeon decayed. Asian men and women stood under Jobs Wanted signs—either smoking or with arms crossed. An old black guy hauled plaid blue luggage from a Chinatown bus toward Canal. Around Hong Ming Market the day turned familiar. A delivery cart had Natty Dread painted down the handle. Camera crews filmed pedestrians passing City Hall.

Raphael giggled into his front-desk phone. He wanted me to sign for boxes addressed to Kristin's former roommate. I told him Justine might be coming to pick these up. Raphael said We're sick of this cabinet not shutting. Things got tense so fast. Soon I was riding the elevator, singing "It Ain't Me Babe," wondering if Raphael watched on the closed-circuit screen.

THURSDAY

At 8:36 a bird I could only think of in relation to grackles fluttered before its mate, sang tirelessly with wings stretched wide. Someone with fingerless gloves jogged along the water boxing air. Someone in noisy shorts pumped as if elbowing through a crowd. Now that sycamores had leaves their yellow tint began tilting the park's overall hue toward summer. Willow reeds helped. Hemlock branches would occasionally shimmer.

Somebody stretched on a blanket, barefoot in slacks. His radio played smooth R&B. Another man had ridden a pink dirt bike to the bench where he slept now: slumped over.

Flushing waterfalls exhilarated me but I only realized it later. I thought about how often I'll spot maple saplings. I wondered if there's something prolific about maples. Robins called from piles of twigs. You are the true carnivores I said. Birders crept around bushy rock. One groaned. From the bridge a huge woodpecker fluttered, flapped off into pines. Ascending The Ravine I came out on a film shoot where everybody wore hooded NYFA sweatshirts. The boy in charge cried Let's clear a path for people— though my frown hadn't meant anything so specific.

At The Loch's edge two men practiced Tae Kwon Do. Both laughed but it looked like good exercise. An elderly couple reassured someone We might not sound convincing but we walk this trail every day. They more or less alternated words.

As I dropped down 96th I passed about 40 bus commuters compressed in a rectangle with no one talking. A woman peddled uphill in khaki shorts, adjusted her handlebars, smoking. I read what I could from a beauty parlor signboard. I tried to imagine a wash-and-set. I considered what's readily noticeable while rushing down Amsterdam: stressed out pigeons, also church signs with verses in marquee letters. San Juan Farmacia had a slot where old men bought lottery tickets. NYCHA workers with masks and brooms startled sparrows picking at cheese.

I absolutely needed a wrist brace or something to alleviate my carpal tunnel syndrome. I hoped for a Kings' Pharmacy since in my mind they're cheapest. I couldn't remember if it's CVS or Duane Reade that's refused to sign a contract with its union for years. In Rite Aid "Joanna" by Kool & the Gang was on and the cashiers wore Islamic headscarves. After circling around a while I apologized for interrupting two Spanish-speaking clerks. The guy on a ladder grimaced and shrugged. Do you have wrist braces? I asked the woman on the floor. Her eyes went opaque. You know like a knee brace I said, squatting. Chec aisle 6 she said.

On the way back I felt cheated, like I always do after buying something, since what I could use the most is skill. I passed someone blowing off his job handing out free tabloids. Instead he talked with a friend. It was probably just shyness. From all the transparent recycling bags it seemed like everybody now owns a paper shredder. Peeking in lobbies I couldn't help wincing at one person steering a tile-scrubber.

One girl asked if we had crossed 108th (street signs above). We talked a bit about disorientation. Another girl carried a garbage bag of worn-out shoes in either hand. A Turkish cleaning woman added nuance to how I picture spring. I think it's crooked, a frail man declared, pointing at the skeletal high-rise. Yeah you're true his companion answered—pointing a finger at the first man's bichon. Police stopped cars amid flashing sirens. There'd been a major accident where Park Drive curves.

On the way through our courtyard I saw someone had swept baby robins pushed from their nests last night. Inside I found Yuki and her sister in the kitchen. I almost opened the bathroom door on a different guest. The hall filled with laughter then surprisingly low voices. The snapping flip-flops made things sassy. Yuki sounded so self-assured.

FRIDAY

With guests here someone's always in the bathroom. While waiting I wrote lists of people to contact before leaving for Berlin. At 9:12 I saw Yuki sitting at her computer but spun around (she looked exhausted). After two nights without alcohol I felt so much happier and had a memory.

More idle teens filled the park than before: it made me glad to be moving. Green bulbs climbed out from The Meer. Koi hovered beside a mossy police barricade. I wondered for the thousandth time if spontaneous rippling on a pond's surface always comes from animals. I decided that the closest man's method of fishing—where you're constantly casting or reeling—fit best with my temperament. In the Lincoln Correction Facility's rooftop cage I thought I saw rows of heads. I pictured inmates eating breakfast up there.

I pledged to pass quickly through the Gardens. Circling Untermeyer Fountain I barely paused. Still, I couldn't help noticing freaked hybrids between Dreamland and Blue Aimable tulips; admitting the Aimables were too bold to be called violet; deciding that stumpy, defective flowers are necessary components of the overall day; sensing stalks rival blossoms for beauty in my unconscious; gasping when colors flushed as I crossed into sun. From The Meer's edge someone called out Tish! then Quiet the fuck down, yo?

Both allées fluttered like a feathery rug. A black boy flapping his clean linen suit made me want to wear white this summer. Half up the Pergola I listened to a songster, wishing I knew more birds' names. On my way down to the South Garden Spring Green tulips glimmered like candles. Don Quixotes proved the depths of pink. Peer Gynts mellowed into dry mauve smolder. Fidelios paused, lemony, preparing to dominate the beds, but late-blooming daffodils pleased me most: Sun Discs, Suzys, Silver Chimes. Someone dragged her suitcase past it all, which I found totally impressive. My cellphone buzzed with untraceable numbers. I hoped it wasn't more bad news about my grandpa.

Meanwhile somebody aimed her cellphone and photographed bronze statues. A plump red cardinal lingered along a fence. I cut through fieldtrips considering how many sexily dressed teachers I'd seen since April (not just stylish but really arousing, and not afraid to return a glance).

A tubular bird like a heron but with thick breasts strode through the reeds—a kingfisher? I followed it. When it started wading I followed some bongos up Lenox, stumbling across a blanket of pirated DVD's, almost stepping on a bottle of Bacardi 40/40 as Levi Stubbs sang Didn't I treat you right now baby, Didn't I?

Through crowds I saw that the chanting came from a chorus dressed in white. I guessed the angelic boy I'd seen earlier was involved in this pageant of spring and gleaming religious children. Two limos passed with headlights on followed by a hearse spilling lurid flowers. A couple dressed with macabre formality (top hat, stilettos) marched ahead of a white carriage drawn by white, black-plumed steeds and a coffin inside the glass encasement marked Owens.

The singers kept repeating a refrain about "forever," which felt really monotonous and electrifying. Most boys mumbled but many girls started clapping with their own momentum independent of the song. I doubted this immodest dead person deserved my contribution to the scene. I turned north past two men wondering something similar. Sure you're *alive*, one told the other, But you *still* ain't got no money.

Along 114th strong Mexicans students struggled fitting a water heater down narrow outdoor steps. On 115th I discovered what's got to be my nearest library. Beyond its courtyard came what sounded like a CUNY commencement ceremony: City College, City Technological College... But by the next block I'd crossed right back to the funeral. From Mt. Horeb Baptist Church's stoop an elegant crowd waved on the approaching choir. Random pedestrians broke into song: For-*ev*-er! and *ev*er! One androgynous adult looked agonized.

I turned south past a clichéd, pony-tailed hippie, smirking above a sign that said Spare Any Change For Pot? At 116th a mural quoted Martin Luther King: On the stairway of religion you don't need to see that whole staircase, you've just got to take that first step. This seemed a paraphrase, a little clumsy for King. Nearby sat a dusty storefront entitled St. Nick's: Video Games, Pool Tables, Candy, Chips, Etc. Someone squatted scratching Lotto tickets, wearing white Stan Smith sneakers without laces, surely crushing his shins. Behind him stood Tropicana cartons with straws. Beside a C-Town white-coated butchers helped the Porky's delivery guy stack dripping boxes. Faded graffiti read FIGHT AIDS / NOT / AIDS PATIENTS.

As he rang up my bananas the owner of Parkview Deli told a girl Get the fuck out I don't want your business. He aggressively fried some eggs. After you help this *dude* you can make my shit she yelled, not directing her words at anybody.

On the street I passed Yuki and her friends (with luggage). Luis and Frankie locked the building next door—I wondered if Mr. Menon bought that one, too.

...Whistler paintings where everything's blue.

MONDAY

Things moved quickly from alarm clock to contacts to kissing Kristin in the elevator. By 8:05 someone wearing pink wanted me to think her dog looked cute. Somebody smoked in a nook in shirtsleeves. It was the time of year I tell people to visit New York, slightly cooler than typical spring.

Car-lot attendants with black bowties leaned against a silver truck talking. A boy and his dad shared a scooter: the younger beaming, the elder in shades. Approaching a snack cart I scanned its shelves for a thought or image to hold onto—nothing.

Accelerating across Murray to avoid cabs catching a fresh green signal I remembered what it felt like to run. I got happy to have skipped the cognac drink I allow myself on Sundays. Just before entering the Church St. post office I glimpsed starry tiles. I passed beneath gridded windows, sensing how spiritual modernism was. There weren't any change of address forms. There were envelopes crammed so the slots seemed full. I despondently consulted display panels. I interrupted a woman installing stamp machines. But she stayed nice about it. I followed, fixated on her rastafari hat. She dug up two forms and gave me both. I thanked her (wondering how I would carry these documents). My wrists hurt more than ever.

I had the annoying sense my shoes were about to come untied and kept staring down. I stopped to read a Times front page. A clerk's question so startled me I jumped back to sidewalk. Amid estuary-like momentum where local foot-traffic and PATH crowds converged I paused to watch people push ahead before their eyes adjusted to aboveground light. Many sneezed. I considered how women from

New Jersey, from most of America outside New York, dress to look attractive from a distance—meaning less subtle hues—though I'm sure class determines color options.

I cut through a Trinity Church rear entrance. Beneath bright sycamores its cemetery flushed. Pink crabapple petals decked some gravestones. I didn't want to read names on mausoleum towers. I read about James Chad departing this world at age 40 on April 4, 1797. I wondered if his life felt long. I thought about how I don't have consistent values.

Dropping into Battery Park I passed the oddly placed Museum of the American Indian, curious if people ever go. Men dragging pretzel carts down to the water bobbed along exaggerating the rhythm of their steps. Slashed tree stumps traced this year's abrupt landscaping. A rollerblader took his socks off, stepped barefoot into business shoes. A turkey or a peacock—a brown-tipped, upright bird— rummaged between fences. Nobody cared.

Where I curved along the Esplanade a square of memorial slabs (New Yorkers who died in WWII?) stood scarred, ready to crack and topple. Queen of Night tulips wavered slightly in a slender row. A park officer coasting past waved to plaid-skirted Jewish girls. Not one acknowl- edged him.

Watching a pudgy sparrow on the river rail I found it wonderful that birds have survived. New Jersey commerce cast searing glares across the Hudson. A mom exiting a bus's face seemed half-scarred red. A pair of joggers argued each other was skinniest. A group of white workmen ate what looked like mango sandwiches. I considered how early they must have started to already be on break. I remembered how pleasant it is to share mornings with your peers, and the muddled self-consciousness afterwards.

In Kowsky Plaza twins strung a volleyball net. A boy on a sailboat turned his face to the light. I wanted to suggest he remove his sunglasses. A water taxi cruised past kicking up wake.

Hurrying now I observed St. John's students sitting silently opposite each other: thinking, not lonely. Someone didn't notice as she stepped towards a sprinkler. This incident about to happen already felt complete. I wanted to detect supple changes all my life. I wanted there to be a point to remembering things. Raphael wouldn't look up from his Daily News.

TUESDAY

I stepped out with no sense of weather. Still not warm enough for shorts. On a second trip across the hall I restrained myself from signaling Luis. I wanted a key for the basement laundry room but couldn't talk because I was about to surge. At 11:06 I hit 110th and mailed my change of address form.

At the corner someone college-aged laughed amid sparrows, stood idle and almost menacing (this explained a lot of strangers' reactions to me). Somebody crouched and sighed, thrilled to photograph the Farmer's Gate. A man sat grinning near a spilled can of Pepsi. A baby heron crept through muck until falling into The Meer chin-first. A woman dropped down steps wearing violet pants, with a violet sweater around the waist, mauve open-toed shoes, mauve blouse and cumbersome lavender purse held tight. When we passed she blinked as if refusing assistance. With my backpack stuffed I could only look south.

Bubbles beneath the waterfall glared like hot white marble. For the first time in months I watched a dog (a retriever puppy) writhe on its back. How you feeling Kate? called out the fun lesbian owner. Someone sensed me watch him stare through branches at sky. He snapped and hurried off (to my regret).

Some branches cast shadows on others, exponentially thickening the foliage. A problem arose behind my left knee; the nerves would flash in a spider-web pattern. As siblings spread along The Loch two tall boys whistled. OK one said, He's coming at you right now. I remembered crayfish. I crossed through the type of sweet rank aroma that makes you wonder where a pet has been.

Where I climbed out from The Ravine kids bunched in red jerseys. When I got higher I saw these were actually blue. Football squads split apart with the females stepping self-consciously. Other girls watched from boulders. Again I felt guilty getting sexual around teachers—who are trained to establish eye contact.

Smog left distant sweeps of buildings looking like a dated postcard. At the first break in Yoshino cherries I paused surrounded by pink. Plodding sounds had been approaching for a while. Just as I turned two Clydesdales passed. Crowds abandoned previous interests and gawked at the horses. To a Japanese couple with many cameras these animals suggested nature not surveillance. Even a Buddhist priest posed smiling.

Someone identical to Kristin's sister hoisted a shrieking infant overhead. I took it as a sign Aime had born her child. I spotted the Polish king's statue—something I always consider good. Four moms scaled benches in aerobic unison, each with a carriage in sight. Tourists stared up at the obelisk behind the Met.

I caught the outer reaches of The Pinetum (my favorite place in the park). After a brief stint through The Ramble I curved along The Boathouse (between usher-type men in tuxedos). From The Drive a British dad said So what kind of birds did we see this morning? With the second species listed (starling) his daughter passed beyond my range.

A cornetist played a song which in movies means Here comes the president. A Columbian family combined preppiness with intense eroticism. I peeked in The Dairy for a map to help me remember but they only stocked sophisticated versions you had to buy. I didn't want to enter The Plaza but looked enough like a tourist to get a free map. A doorman asked Can I *help* you sir? I'm staying here and want a park map I said. Sir? the guard responded. The Plaza's *closed*.

So I continued south, confused by businessmen with partial mohawks. I slowed to read the Times front page. I sensed how for five years I've been stopping, awaiting good news. A fashionable man's boot heels clicked: a masculinity I haven't dealt with yet. Noon bells filled my attention as I crossed 54th. Women's breasts in oxford shirts seemed to reach out just for me, just like in adolescence.

Three men slid into separate lunch booths talking (each a bit bewildered by his salad). For the first time this season I crossed into shade. With the president's song still in my head I turned into school, into the library stacks, my favorite favorite place I guess, where twenty-thousand shelved titles looked right.

WEDNESDAY

More bad sleep, with squares of light that slip through Kristin's drapes intensifying and my balls scrunched. Still I crossed Greenwich just to smile at the picketing teacher's union. By 8:46 I'd focused on a woman's clean bare heels. Nothing seemed more urban than sandals.

I had to do something about the Fanny Howe book I was carrying; my wrists couldn't take the pressure. When I tucked the book in the back of my jeans one girl winced. Along the water I passed a security guard in nylon jacket, shirt and tie—each a different blue. She moved so slow it looked like exercise. Rounding Robert Wagner Park I spotted a returning ferry.

Soon I began weaving through men flashing watches. A blonde with a jump rope made some sassy comment. I kept smiling, waiting to understand what she'd said. I rushed toward Whitehall Terminal ready to sprint if the crowds swelled. The new lobby looked dingy and easy to love. I barely noticed sledgehammers.

Boarding the Guy V. Molinari I reasoned that this trip could count in my walks if I never sat, stayed outside and never read the Fanny Howe. The boxy overlap of Brooklyn/Manhattan bridges reminded me of Frank Lloyd Wright windows. Downtown looked like any financial district from the freeway (Hartford especially). White wooden towers gleamed on Governor's Island. Groups of white suds drifted past. The hurricane deck's other passenger frowned. It's *cold* out here. I *know* I said. That's all it took to get her giggling. She wore a neon pink sweater, yellow neon flats. I noticed I'd been trembling.

Assuming the non-ocean side would be less windy I switched, coming out on cranes across Kill Van Kull. For now there weren't any ships to tend. I wondered what such monstrous stature and strength meant to previous generations. I decided there's no better sound than a buoy's bell. I stared down at the shadow of a flag, a pipe shaped like a megaphone, my bent figure. I'd never seen the large stone church just west of St. George Terminal.

I cut through couples, considered them a hindrance. We had eighteen minutes before the next boat left. A muscular crewcut man confided They tell me Be *safe*. Get home safe...all that shit. I thought of how the poet Joshua Beckman remains the one person I know on Staten Island. I hurried through a loop around the Borough Hall, waved at the public library, read the sign Baker Square Park and the street signs Hyatt and Stuyvesant.

Pressed into a crowd boarding the Andrew Barberi I ended up beside Joshua Beckman (on his phone). I said hi. He seemed uncomfortable. As we pulled out the Verranzano Bridge reminded me of Whistler paintings where everything's blue. Traffic became a darker blue pushing across it. For this return trip I focused on glassy stretches. I stood packed in with girls playing hooky: some bragging, others paranoid.

Girls squealed inside a bus on Battery Place. A man with a microphone revved them up. A separate girl in tight green Veterinary Volunteer t-shirt stepped last from a cab. Her parents looked calcified. They paused beneath a Dutch flag post offered in good faith to the British around 1660.

Kids overran Wagner Park kicking balls much bigger than themselves, dressed like millionaires. Tugboats led barges labeled Buchanan which probably carry coal. People sauntered by with limbs loose but I still had ferry drafts caught in my sweater. A petite jogger all in black checked me out as she shook her quads. I wondered why I also wore all black. I pledged to carry my Fanny Howe book the rest of the way, however painful, so as not to further damage it, since it was from the public library. Bellhops outside the Residence Suites practiced kicking doors down and pointing pistols. Crossing Barclay I knew I'd never been so trim, sensed I'm happiest small, considered how appropriate this will become if space travel gets cheap. Finally I nodded at Raphael who choked a bit, drooling coffee.

THURSDAY

I shaved before leaving since the Gardens weren't open yet. I decided it's warm enough for shorts when you say it is. At 7:53 I stepped through a puddle, kicking water up one ankle, uncertain what was rain. With thin socks on I didn't know how to carry my keys or phone. Situating both in underwear elastic I vowed to soon find another solution.

Just ahead the tall Brazilian blocked The Meer. When we drew parallel her profile looked cracked. A woman exasperated by a mutt caused further problems flailing its leash. Cars turned on lights against pre-storm darkness. A mom and daughter passed riding an old tandem Schwinn with the girl only pedaling when she thought about it. All together the willows grass and daffodil husks heaved.

Already lilacs overwhelmed The Gardens. I couldn't tell if pink, magenta and white varieties gave off different scents. I got curious if a lot of garden time can inoculate allergies. Someone read with a French-English dictionary in his lap on a bench along the North Parterre. It seemed the perfect place for that. As waning Dreamlands rocked in wind I wondered which would survive the storm.

In the South Garden the Elegant Ladies had bloomed, the last of the great tulips. I scanned the general decay a couple minutes. I saw new growth enliven perennial beds. Prickly, burr-like bulbs swung about. Somebody bald stalked the Woodland Slope—weird, bare-chested, like it was a confessional. I wondered if snowdrops appear each season (or between seasons). Exiting from one allée I wanted to cry at how smooth its stones had set.

I turned past what in winter seemed a soupy fenced-off garbage pit. Since then the water evaporated, leaving dozens of 40-ounce bottles in sand. I kept remembering how in 7th grade everyone pulled down each other's shorts. The best shop I saw was Hielos En Bloque. Within shapes stood visible but dark: storm light.

Parking tickets stuck to a sewer grate. It's so fun to watch people toss those things. I wondered why I make a mental note whenever I spot a new post office. I crossed the F.D.R. thinking I'll next see this river in final descent from Germany. Somebody with a cigarette behind his ear put a half-burned one out against the rail. For the first time I reflected on a student's essay (about public smoking). Torn clouds beyond the Triborough Bridge cast hues made ugly by the industrial context, gross even, like a Christian Realist painting. Lamps lit Riker's Island.

In the Thomas Jefferson Park Dog Run sat one man (without pet). This inspired me to take the jogging track. Sprinters clotted outer lanes while inside walkers commiserated. In a fenced plot a boy played foursquare with the girls. I've been really wanting to abandon whatever traits of a paranoid personality structure I possess, like Stalin and billions of other people. It seemed so much easier around these kids. The Church of the Holy Tabernacle's sign read STILL ALIVE IN 2005 / THE YEAR OF EVANGELISM! I thought No, that's not the year it feels like to me.

I cut through projects I couldn't name—a white guy in skimpy Diadora shorts. I crossed what I think were Union Settlement Houses, passed more young men than on any other walk. At the James Weldon Johnson Homes rat-poison warnings posted to trees turned white. Backboards had graffiti but not any rims. An arrow pointed down a paved path above the caption STRIVE. I headed through the gate, past a statue of someone with orphans in his arms, across Third Ave. and through a second set of Johnson projects to a sculpture of ballerinas reaching up for a bronze sphere. One dancer's feet had been spray-painted. Somebody left a LaCroix can between them. Still in the surprising lush it felt hard to feel hopeless (I mean, I guess, about politics).

Pausing beneath commuter trains I scanned a month of tabloids and remembered most headlines. The Taft Homes started and I took these to 5th. On my own block a flyer read: Have you recently known jail / Out in last 90 days / Finding it hard? / If you answered yes to all the above call Operation Exodus.

Abandoned cabinets looked worth keeping if it wasn't for the rain. By the time I'd crossed our courtyard ubiquitous drilling had begun.

FRIDAY 5.13

I biked around too much last night, ate an extra cheese sandwich. I woke from a religious prison nightmare and couldn't get back to sleep. When I stepped out at 10:30 it felt cool and dry. I was wearing pants again. The first person to pass looked like if he wasn't pushing a wheelchair he would have had to sit in one.

An old guy exited a grocery tossing sneakers. He caught up with the shoes and stomped. Someone selling things from a blanket called Damn it Ronnie, don't lose your temper. Someone else shouted Lucy! right into my ear. On sidewalk outside Captain's (seafood place) ice cream melted in a perfect square. From his station wagon at 124th a man sold Etta James and Jimmy Smith bootlegs. He hadn't been there in April.

After feeling like a failure a couple blocks I decided there was no way for these walks to include upper upper Manhattan—it would have wrecked my memory to ride a train. I pledged to tomorrow cross Central Park then the Queensborough Bridge into Queens. My left wrist ached. Fingers curled. Lilacs bloomed in vacant lots. One man's voice rose above the rest: What was their *last* war about? *Price* control!

At 136th one-way streets converged, confusing my sense of balance. An adult fired an uzi-shaped squirt gun near me. Bang bang bang bang he said. Someone sat on a pipe, his leg hooked to another, so that he could both stretch and read the paper. I was steaming in sun but wouldn't stop to take my sweater off.

From 147th I saw Yankee Stadium's scoreboard constantly change. Close by stood a hangar of MTA busses. The drivers looked poised in brown sunglasses and leather. An M1 departed for the East Village.

An attractive woman tossed a Fanta bottle. She said the home they'd put her in had a 9 o'clock curfew. Behind a fence a sign read Rand Engineering. I wondered if this was part of the Rand Corporation. Weaving through stale dog turds and broken glass I wondered what the Rand Corporation does. The Delano Village complex had a run-down Met Foods with Domino's Pizza trucks parked outside.

I continued north, sensing public space. I pushed on to Bradhurst and Jackie Robinson Park, circling the castle, convinced it housed a swimming pool. I passed a Mexican man's grocery cart from which whole peeled pineapples dangled on sticks. The lush made me want to not be so busy this summer. On my way down Edgecombe a bumper sticker bragged School of War / Vietnam University.

In St. Nick's Park boys painted handball courts. One let a giant roll of tape unspool twenty feet into his partner's grasp. One woman yelled You forgot about *Paul*....He *never* listens to what I have to say! Nobody sat on the bench beside her. I paused impressed when, on the bench after that, a fat woman stretched way past her foot.

Around 128th I read about Green Thumb getting launched by activists in the 70s. I sensed strange new platforms affixed to every stoplight. I noticed people perched in cardboard boxes above the hydrants. A gorgeous Salvadorian girl stared while her mom readjusted her stocking. A black man flipped dry-cleaning across his shoulder. Our neighborhood felt hip and gay like London.

Along 35 West a woman shook her cane. As I turned in she moaned Not near *my* building; I can't believe the extent of this shit! She pointed at something. I didn't feel like looking.

Instead of sprinting up stairs as I always do—often wondering why—I experimented with the elevator key.

When the green light flashed I pressed 2. But the elevator sank to the basement and just sat a long time. It opened on a red rug rolled into shadows. With footsteps coming I pushed Close Door twice. This time I made it up and (as I crossed the hall) heard Yuki start the shower.